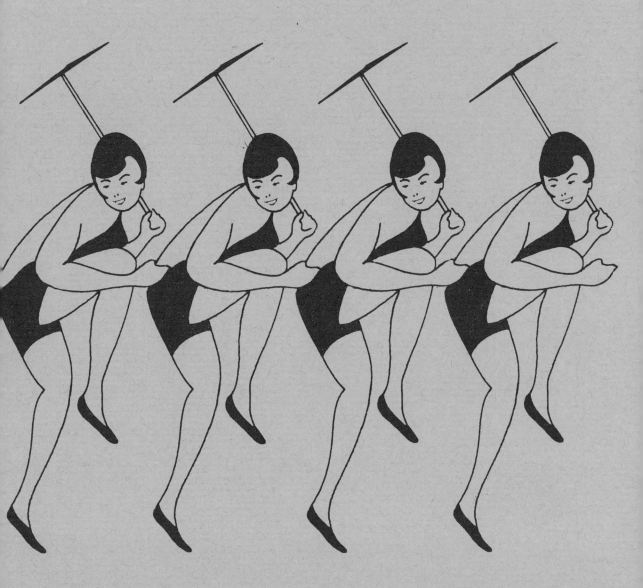

REVUE

REVUE

A Story in Pictures

by

RAYMOND MANDER & JOE MITCHENSON

Foreword by NOËL COWARD

' . . . to hold, as 'twere, the mirror up to nature; to show virtue
her own feature, scorn her own image, and the very age and
body of the time his form and pressure.'

Hamlet

Taplinger Publishing Company
New York

First published in the United States in 1971 by
TAPLINGER PUBLISHING CO., INC.
New York, New York

Library of Congress Catalog Card Number: 76-163477
ISBN 0-8008-6789-0

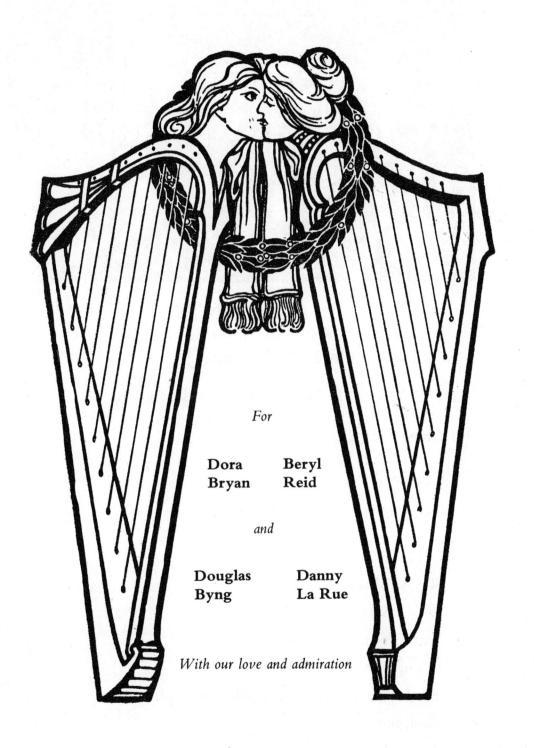

For

**Dora   Beryl
Bryan   Reid**

and

**Douglas   Danny
Byng   La Rue**

With our love and admiration

CONTENTS

Foreword by NOËL COWARD

I have been connected with, or written words and music for, or acted in a great many revues through most of the years that might be described as the Golden Age of Revue. I have seen almost every revue worth mentioning in London, Paris and New York from *Hullo, Rag-time!* in 1912 to *Oh! Calcutta!* in 1970. I walked out of the latter half-way through the first half exclaiming clearly though, polite to the last, *sotto voce*, 'This is insupportable!' to the remaining three of my party of four. They, reliable friends, reported next day that the *pas de deux* in the second half had been lovely but that in their opinion I hadn't missed much.

Writing for revue is a difficult, delicate art, as is directing revue and both these arts seem, in 1971, almost to be lost. A sketch for a revue must be quick, sharp, funny (or sentimental) and to the point, with a good, really good black-out line. Whether the performers are naked or wearing crinolines is quite beside the point; the same rule applies.

Where are the revue writers of yesteryear, and where, oh where, are the directors, the great directors—Albert de Courville, Sir Alfred Butt, André Charlot and Sir Charles B. Cochran?

The last writers I can call to mind who really knew how to do it were Arthur Macrae and Jonathan Miller, Peter Cook, Alan Bennett and Dudley Moore, who supplied their own brilliant material for *Beyond the Fringe*.

As for directors, Danny La Rue's revue is still running triumphantly at the Palace, directed by Freddie Carpenter, with, I suspect, more than a few suggestions by Danny himself. Three cheers for them both. Then there is Robert Nesbitt. Any show put on by Bob Nesbitt is well dressed, beautifully lit, entertaining and swift. And he knows about Running Order.

I first learned about the bugbear, Running Order, that endlessly fascinating and always essential aspect of revue, from André Charlot when I appeared in and wrote much of the material for *London Calling* in 1923. He would have the names of all the numbers in the revue printed on separate cards, place them on his desk and then, as though playing Patience, juggle with them and go on moving them about, shifting them again and again until he was satisfied that they were in the right running order. The finale of the first half would already have been agreed upon but all the numbers leading up to it had to build, and build to the number *before* the finale and that number, whatever it was, had to be sure-fire. The second number in the second half was, still is, and always will be, terribly important. It has to be so strong, or so funny, or so spectacular or whatever, that the audience, including by then the stragglers from the bar, will settle back comfortably in their seats, happy in the knowledge that the second half is going to be even more brilliant than the first.

All this can be settled with the cards fairly amicably. Then the fun begins. 'You can't possibly change the set from So And So straight into So And So.' 'Gertie couldn't *possibly* make the change from tweeds at the end of the sketch into deep evening dress for the beginning of her big number.' And so on and so on; more juggling of the cards until all is set and all will run smoothly.

This can still be done, present day directors please note, with, first, good material—songs, sketches and dances; then, stars or star personalities if you are lucky enough to find them; taste, tact and endless patience from the director and, never never forget, the right running order.

Some of my stauncher friends and fans, now dwindling in number, thanks to the Great Reaper, still maintain that all these right ingredients miraculously came together in *This Year of Grace* which was produced by C. B. Cochran and every word and note of which was written by me. It was, so they say, the most perfect, the wittiest, the most beautiful, glamorous, funniest revue ever produced. I have always loved and respected revue as a medium and I should be proud, so very very proud, if the few friends left who saw *This Year of Grace* are right.

I feel sure that all those who love revue will join me in thanking Raymond Mander and Joe Mitchenson for this book; for bringing back in words and pictures so many exciting, happy, magical evenings in the theatre. (And some, let's face it, not so magical.) It is a comprehensive, lovingly detailed and—as always with Ray and Joe—accurate History of Revue.

The Story of Revue

J. R. PLANCHÉ

Revue, as the name implies, is of French ancestry. Like all the best and most cherished of British theatrical institutions, from melodrama to farce, it has been assimilated and adapted 'from the French' with or without permission! Larousse Vol. V (1932), the French encyclopaedia, says:

'Revue, originally called "end of the year review", is a form of theatrical production which aims to show a succession of scenes in dialogue and song representing such incidents or individuals as have preoccupied the public to a greater or lesser extent during the course of the year. Adam de la Halle's *Jeu de la feuillée*, dating from the middle ages (1262), could be said to belong to this category, but in fact for the origins of revue one need look back no further than two hundred years. The theatres of the old (Paris) fairs witnessed its earliest developments, under various names. Revues began to be really popular in the reign of Louis Philippe (1830-1848), when the Cogniard brothers, among others, distinguished themselves by their continued work in this line for the Théâtre de la Porte-Saint-Martin. All Paris wanted to see their *Iles Marquises* or their amusing parody of progress carried to extremes, *l'an 1841 et l'an 1941*. In 1848 and 1849 there was an absolute deluge of revues, including *la Foire aux idées*, *Suffrage Premier*, *la Propriété c'est le vol*, *les Grenouilles qui demandent un roi*, etc. The period of the Second Empire (1852-1870) suffered no lack of this form of entertainment. *Gare l'eau!* at the Bobino (1862) and *Bu qui s'avance* at the Folies-Marigny were notable examples. The third Republic (from 1870) saw the rise of a generation that was especially rich in revue writers, such as Clairville, Burani, Busnach, Blum and Toché, Albert Wolff, and later Gavault, Vély, de Cottens, de Flers, de Gorsse, Rip, Bousquet, Jeanson, etc. Music hall, in its later development, gave birth to a particular kind known as "spectacular" revue, which is merely a series of tableaux produced with a lavish display of scenery and costumes.'

An English equivalent concisely defines Revue as 'a term of French origin, used to describe a survey, mainly satiric, of contemporary events, with songs, sketches, burlesques, monologues and so on. No satisfactory English term has ever been found for this mixture, and the French continues in use.'

This description can also be roughly applied to the repertoire of the handful of solo entertainers who appeared in London and the provinces before any English experiments in revue were staged.

No better idea of the style of the embryo days of these entertainments, and the subsequent early revues, can be captured than in quoting the contemporary bills, descriptions and notices which reflect their impact on the audiences of their own day, and are in no way influenced by hindsight.

Of the principal ingredients of revue, those of burlesque and satire—social, topical or political—have long been current coinage of the British theatre. 'The Burlesque Tradition' has been excellently recorded by V. C. Clinton-Baddeley in his book of that title. It was Henry Fielding's political satire in his plays and ballad operas at the Little Theatre in the Haymarket, continually attacking the Government in general, and Walpole in particular, which caused the introduction of stage censorship in 1737. Also Pantomime, as formulated by John Rich early in the eighteenth century, by the time of Grimaldi had become an annual entertainment and a particularly English institution, As David Mayer's *The English Pantomime 1806-1836* points out:

'. . . it reflected and recorded the social, economic, political, and aesthetic issues of the time and, in the face of vigilant and tenacious censorship and chaotic licensing laws, was the only dramatic form to oppose the reigning follies and to serve as a vehicle for social comment and satire.'

Fielding was followed by Samuel Foote (1720-1777) at the same Theatre in 1747 who gave entertainments mimicking his fellow actors and public characters, both solo and in plays, causing him to be dubbed 'the English Aristophanes.'

Yet another, Charles Dibdin (1745-1813), an actor, singer, composer, playwright and manager, became so quarrelsome with his fellow managers that he was almost forced to appear alone in the provinces in 1788. His mixture of his own songs interspersed with monologues and topical sketches was to bring him undying fame as the first truly versatile one man entertainer. He came to London the following year and in 1791 opened his own Sans Souci Theatre in the Strand with *Private Theatricals; or, Nature in Nubibus*. A contemporary advertisement says:

'This Amusement will embrace a large field of objects, impossible to be enumerated in an advertisement or handbill. Among a variety of other subjects, Matrimony— Lady-writing —Theatricals—Opera — Speculation—Tippling— The Perversion of Epithets—Punning—Curiosity—Man-Hunting—Queering— The Rights of Man—Charity—Alliteration—Perfumery—Philanthropy and Gratitude, will not escape observation. The songs will come in the following succession.

Part I. True Wisdom—The Rara Avis—Conjugal Comfort—Poor Peg—Nothing but Drunk—The Sailor's Consolation—A Mock Recitative and Duetto.

Part II. Tack and Tack—Virtue—Tantivy—The Sailor's Return—The Waggoner—The Soldier's Last Retreat—Life's a Pun—Bill Bobstay.

Part III. The Drummer—The Beggar—Roses and Lilies—The Lucky Escape—Meum and Tuum—Jack's Gratitude, or The Royal Tar—The Sultan and The Wag.

'The whole is written and composed, and will be spoken, sung and accompanied by Mr. Dibdin.'

He moved from the Strand to a second Sans Souci in Leicester Place in 1796, remaining there till he retired in 1804.

This form of one-man revue was even more successfully exploited by Charles

Mathews (1776-1835), a famous comedian who 'went solo' in 1808. His *At Homes* under various titles were a popular entertainment in London, on tour and in America for over twenty years. He seems to have been an accomplished writer, actor, singer, mimic, impersonator, ventriloquist and quick-change artist all rolled into one and his varied programmes fall into the class we would now term *An Evening with ——*.

Charles Mathews senior (his son Charles James Mathews comes later into the story) had a pupil and protégé, Frederick Yates (1795-1842), who took over the Adelphi Theatre in partnership with Daniel Terry in 1825. Their first success, *The Pilot* by Edward Fitzball, which opened on 31 October had different after-pieces, and on 12 December the current afterpiece was changed to what was called on the playbill in the fashion of the time:

A New, Grand, Mock-Heroical, Allegorical, Operatical, Melo-Dramatical
Magical, (Any Thing but Tragical) Burletta.
In one Act, founded on Fact.
Entitled
SUCCESS!
or,
A HIT, IF YOU LIKE IT.
With a *New Scene*, which being impossible to describe, must be seen to be appreciated—nevertheless the Painter intends it to represent
THE PALACE OF FASHION
Somewhere at the *West End of the Town*, exhibiting, among a Variety of emblematical Peculiarities, all the Architecture that ever was known, from the Parthenon at Athens to the Patent-Shot Manufactory on the Surrey side of the Thames, and a great deal that never will be known, except by the Visitors of the Adelphi Theatre, and adorned with Statues of the most celebrated Exquisites, ancient and modern, from the Apollo Belvidere and the Medicean Venus, to her of Hottentot, and the "Anatomie Vivante."
The Scene by Mr. Walker. The Dresses by Mr. Godbee and Assistants.
The Properties by Mr. Woodyer. The Music selected and arranged by Mr. G. B. Herbert.

No author is credited but it was by James Robertson Planché who in his reminiscences, *Recollections and Reflections*, published in 1872, tells us:

'My theatrical labours in the year 1825 terminated with the production at the Adelphi, then under the management of Messrs. Terry and Yates, of a one-act piece on the 12 December, entitled *Success! or, a Hit, if You Like It*, which I only mention because it was the first attempt in this country to introduce that class of entertainment so popular in Paris called *Revue*, and of which, with one solitary exception, I believe I have been the sole contributor to the English stage. This rather bold experiment, illustrated by the talent of Wrench, Terry, Yates, T. P. Cooke, Mrs. Yates, Mrs. Fitzwilliam, and other deservedly favourite performers, was a "success" so satisfactory that it encouraged me to follow it up as occasion presented itself: and if I am any judge of my own works, these *pièces de circonstance*, though inevitably ephemeral from their nature, are amongst the most creditable of my dramatic compositions.'

The 'new' entertainment was revised and kept up to date and ran over fifty performances. A contemporary critic in *The Weekly Dramatic Register* (24 December) says:

[3]

'Adelphi.—This little Theatre seems increasing in popularity every successive evening. They produced on Monday, after the Burletta of *The Pilot*, a sort of nondescript piece, of considerable merit, entitled *Success! or, a Hit, if You Like It*, which our limits would only permit us to notice in yesterday's number, but which we think deserving of every publicity we can afford it. The plot, if plot it can be called, is of an allegorical nature; the scene opens in the Temple of Fashion; that autocrat of the civilized world, personated by Mr. Wrench, is pestered by the application of a variety of dramatic suitors for the hand of his fair daughter, Success, (Mrs. Fitzwilliam). To assist him in his choice, he calls in the various periodicals, (ourselves of course amongst the number) who form a conclave in an interior apartment; each candidate for 'Success' is previously introduced to the Princess alone, to plead his claim; they appear in the following order—Zamiel, (Mr. T. P. Cooke) this part, of course, would not admit of much brilliancy, but afforded Mrs. Fitzwilliam an opportunity of singing a capital comic song, ridiculing the excessive rage for the Jäger Chorus, which was unanimously encored. Mr. Yates, as Mathews—an imitator with several capital puns. Mr. Reeve, as Junius Brutus, who gave us a few sentences *à la* Kean, with great ruth. Mr. Terry, as Mephistophiles, was, as the bills state, himself; he introduced a pretty allusion to the fallen fortunes of a late favorite performer, which, coupled with the letters that have lately appeared in the American papers, produced a strong sensation. Amongst the follies of the day, Policinello, of course, made his appearance. Reeve's Paul Pry was Liston all over. The fair lady, Success, appeared inclined to bestow her favours on the representative of Mazurier, but, after a violent squabble between the candidates and umpires, her father, Fashion, interferes, and, as might be expected, bestows Success on the candidate of his own establishment—*Long Tom Coffin*.'

The following year, on 3 April, Yates himself tried a solo evening *à la* Mathews at the Adelphi. He too was successful and later toured and added other programmes to his repertoire. The partnership with Terry was dissolved, owing to his financial difficulties, and Yates was joined by Mathews in partnership in April 1828. The two friends were to inaugurate a series of joint *At Homes* on 30 April 1829. Mathews later appeared alone in several annual entertainments until 1834 when, though in bad health, he went once again to America but returned home to die the following year. Yates remained at the Adelphi until he died in 1842.

* * * * * *

Though not quite in the same style Frances Maria Kelly (1790-1882) appears to have been the first one woman actress-entertainer. She opened at the Strand Subscription Theatre (near Somerset House) in January 1833 with a mixed programme of songs knitted together with her theatrical memories, but her big triumphs lay in her 'invented' characters. She moved to her own little Theatre and Dramatic Academy, which she opened in 1835, in Dean Street, Soho, (later the Royalty) where she appeared in a revival of her *Dramatic Recollections and Studies of Character* in 1841.

The part of Fanny Kelly's entertainment relevant to the story of revue is her character 'Mrs. Parthian.' Her biographer, Basil Francis, tells us:

'Dressed in a grey wig, a voluminous silk dress, cap, spectacles and shawl, she walked slowly on to the stage, leaning on her ebony stick, and settled herself comfortably in an armchair. She would then lean forward and in a vague, confidential manner gossip to her audience of her recollections of bygone actors and personalities and events of her own youth as a travelling actress. The script of "Mrs. Parthian" was attributed to John Hamilton Reynolds, although Crabb Robinson writing in his Diary under date 31 January felt sure that Lamb wrote at least part of it. He quotes one of the 'Parthian' jokes as being in Lamb's own peculiar style. Mrs. Parthian is trying to recall "Gentleman" Smith " . . . His name was Adam Smith and he wrote some pretty songs on political economy and people used to whisper about his addresses having been rejected—I forget by whom, but it was someone at Drury Lane . . . " Crabb Robinson corrects himself later in his Diaries and states that Reynolds was definitely the author of the text—but one cannot help thinking from the above example that Lamb had at least some hand in the composition.'

The playbills gave no credit for the authorship of her material but it is known she wrote much of it herself. Basil Francis, a confirmed Elian, goes on to say:

'Some of her introductory "patter" has an unmistakable Elian ring, in particular the delicious "dig" at Drury Lane and the wonder-dog Carlo. Carlo was a magnificent Newfoundland who appeared nightly under Sheridan's management, to leap into a real stream and save a child from drowning in the production of *The Caravan; or, The Driver and his Dog*. Carlo was the talk of the town in the early years of the century, and Lamb had not forgotten, so he made Miss Kelly tell the story of the proprietor of a caravan of wild beasts who applied to Drury Lane for free seats at the theatre for himself and his *fellow-professionals*.'

'Mrs. Parthian' has the true satirical revue ring about her in the style which later became known as the "Poison Ivy" tradition.

James Robertson Planché who claims, rightly, to have brought Revue to London was a man of immense and varied talents. Born in 1796 of Huguenot descent he lived until 1880. During that period he was the author of plays, opera libretti, both adaptations and originals, countless pantomimes, burlesques, burlettas and extravaganzas, the latter alone published in five volumes.

He was musical director at Vauxhall Gardens, an artist and costume designer; (he was the first to dress Shakespeare in correct historical costume when he worked with Charles Kemble in 1823 on the revival of *King John*). He was the major influence behind the scenic reforms of Madame Vestris at the Olympic Theatre in the eighteen-thirties which made stage history. His book on costume was for many years a standard work and his interest in heraldry led him eventually to the exalted position of Somerset Herald at the Royal College of Heralds. In his plays, and in the press, he campaigned for a home for the national drama and paradoxically he was instrumental in gaining reforms in the laws governing theatrical copyright and giving protection to dramatists, though he himself was, as were most of his contemporaries, a constant pillager from the French! It would seem his introduction of revue, though successful, was a little before its time as the experiment was not repeated immediately, and the work of Yates and Mathews held the field.

[5]

It was not till 1838 that Planché returned to something similar, this time for Mathews's son, Charles James Mathews, and his newly married wife, Madame Vestris. The author tells us in his *Recollections* that the favourable reception of *Success* 'induced me to make a second attempt to naturalise it thirteen years afterwards, when Madame Vestris took her farewell at the Olympic, on her departure for America: but in the latter instance it was specially a *pièce d'occasion*, and the majority of the allusions necessarily personal'.

Of *The Drama's Levee; or, a Peep at the Past*, (16 April 1838), a contemporary critic says:

'We have already said that *The Drama's Levee* is the best of the Easter novelties, but we have yet to add that it is decidedly the best piece of the kind that was ever brought out. It abounds with *wit* without absurdity, *satire* without ill-nature, and smart touches at the existing abuses of the drama without one spark of injustice. Added to this, the splendour in which it has been got up equals any former effort of the sort at this theatre, and the expense incurred must have been enormous. The title of the piece unfolds its nature, *The Drama* (most admirably played by Mrs. Orger) being awakened from a lengthened slumber, summons the representatives of the different theatres to inform her of what is going on in the theatrical world. These are accompanied by *Praise* and *Censure*, (Madame Vestris and Mr. Bland,) whose remarks are full of point and *double entendre;* the *legitimate* and *illegitimate* sons of the drama also attend; the first dressed in a Roman habit, and the second in a dress half harlequin's and half that of a Spanish grandee. They, however, begin to squabble the moment they appear, and ultimately the natural son *un*-naturally drives his brother from the place. Specimens of the recent productions of the different theatres are now presented, not omitting the *Gnome Fly*, which recently buzzed in the public ear at the Adelphi. This gives occasion for some admirable sarcasms on the part of *Censure*, which was one of the best played parts in the piece; but nowhere is the lash inflicted more stingingly than on the desecration of the Surrey—that spot over which the acting of an Elliston, and the united genius of a Shakespeare and a Scott had flung a blaze—by the introduction of *Jim Crow*. The lament by *Praise* of that circumstance was sung to the air of the song itself, and was one of the most exquisite things we ever saw enacted. Madame Vestris threw her best abilities (which are always first-rate) into the effort, and drew a rapturous *encore*. Nothing could have surpassed her manner of acquitting herself; her singing was slow and plaintive, while scorn, contempt, anger, and sorrow, were expressively delineated. The execution of the following stanza was a burst of real histrionic genius:

'Where Walter Scott and Elliston
Had just begun to grow,
It was a blot on such a spot
To jump Jim Crow.'

The *Drama* is now invited to make a personal inspection of the Olympic, and attends for the purpose of witnessing '*A Dream of the Future*.' But at this moment the great American sea serpent summons Madame Vestris to his shores, and the piece ends with an allegorical display, representing the chief characters for which Madame has been famed. The effect of this was very beautiful. Before the falling

[6]

of the curtain, Madame Vestris stepped forward and delivered a poetic address, in which she spoke of her intended and now regretted departure for America. On the first night this drew tears not only from herself, but from many of her auditors.'

Nothing further was tried until April 1844 when, for the Theatre Royal Haymarket, under the management of Ben Webster, Planché wrote 'An entirely new, original, occasional, and local extravagance', *The Drama at Home! or, an Evening with Puff*. Of this the author says:

'At the Haymarket the scope was wider, and in reviewing the popular productions at other houses and the various exhibitions and entertainments which had attracted public attention during the current season, I found opportunities for expressing my humble opinion on theatrical affairs in general, which, however open to correction, were as honestly entertained as, I trust, they were inoffensively promulgated.

'*The Drama at Home!* produced on Easter Monday, 1844, comprised in its cast, Charles James Mathews, James Bland, Miss Priscilla Horton, and Mrs. Glover! I confess, it was with some timidity I saw that noble actress enter the green-room in obedience to a call for the reading of the "new burlesque"! But great was my pride and gratification to observe that she enjoyed every line of it, and received the part assigned to her without the slightest hesitation.'

The Illustrated London News comments:

'On Monday last the entertainments called *Used Up* and *Grist to the Mill*, introduced, or rather *reproduced*, Mr. and Mrs. Mathews on those boards. The novelty of the evening was a new extravaganza by Planché, entitled *The Drama at Home! or, an Evening with Puff*. It is one of those hybrid monstrosities which accelerates the fall of the decadent temple, whose utter ruin it would fain deplore, yet throws, by the help of caricature, a contempt upon that which hitherto had been held sacred. The *Drama* (personified by Mrs. Glover) is discovered in the opening scene, all disconsolate amidst the *débris* of the fane in which she was once worshipped. Her orphan children—*Hamlet*, *Ophelia*, the *Ghost*, *Macbeth*, &c.—all attempt to condole with their mourning parent. At length *Mr. Puff* (Mr. C. Mathews) suddenly appears from a trap, and succeeds in dispelling (for a while) the Muse's fears. She takes new courage, and once more "In vain hope seats herself upon a throne".

'A motley procession is then made to pass before her, caricaturing the productions of other theatres, and insinuating, or rather asserting, that the home of the Legitimate Drama is the Haymarket House. We very much question whether legitimate drama is not involved in a life interest with legitimate actors, and as we have a plentiful lack of them, or we might say a nearly total want of them, our fears are that the lady herself will not pay us a visit in our days.'

These so-called burlettas or extravaganzas were termed 'Easter Pieces' as by this period it had become the custom to present this style of entertainment for the Easter holidays and when based on similar fairy tale or legendary subjects as were pantomimes, the titles are apt to cause confusion in the modern mind.

It was in 1847 (to open on 5 April), that Planché again wrote an 'Easter Piece' for Webster, this time called prophetically *The New Planet! or, Harlequin out of Place* and described as 'an entirely New and Original Classical, Astronomical, Quizzical, Polytechnical, Experimental, Operational, Pantomimical EXTRAVAGANZA'.

The Illustrated London News on 3 April, before it opened, said:

'This clever author has this time abandoned the romances of fairy history, of which he has been time out of mind the chronicler, and produced one of those pieces known at the French theatres as a *revue*. The present piece will commence with a meeting of the different planets in the star-chamber of the new one, with their transit from that locality to 'London by Night'. The first appearance of Mr. Buckstone, in the character of *Harlequin* will, no doubt, be a great feature of this scene. We are next carried through the Polytechnic Institution, with its gun cotton lectures and other wonders: the Egyptian Hall with its opposition nigger Serenaders, the Haunt of the Wilis, with the different Giselles from the Opera, Drury Lane, the Adelphi, the Princess's, &c.: with some hard hitting on both sides at the rival Operas; and the extravaganza winds up with Harlequin's Tableaux Vivants, by various living statues of celebrity, and the enthronization of the new planet.'

This would appear to be one of the earliest contemporary references to the word *revue* as a name for this style of entertainment.

After another gap Planché returned once more to his pet subject:

'I had all along, however, continued writing for the stage, contributing a *pièce de circonstance* for the opening of the Haymarket, under the management of Mr. Buckstone, 28th March, 1853, entitled *Mr. Buckstone's Ascent of Mount Parnassus*, a sort of travesty of Albert Smith's famous entertainment, *The Ascent of Mont Blanc*, then in the height of its popularity [at the Egyptian Hall in Piccadilly].

'In the *Ascent of Mount Parnassus*, which was a species of *Revue*, I introduced a scene representing the room at the Egyptian Hall fitted up for Smith's entertainment aforesaid, and in which the popular entertainer himself was personated by Mr. Caulfield, of the Haymarket company. I had previously asked and received Smith's permission to take this liberty with him, which was most good-naturedly accorded by that genial artist, with whom I had been long on terms of intimacy, and who felt assured that he had nothing to fear from any use I should make of his name or his property.

'He entered indeed into the fun of the thing with such spirit that he determined to act the scene himself some night without apprising Buckstone of his intention. Accordingly one evening, having privately intimated his intention to Mrs. Fitzwilliam, his own performance terminating at ten, affording him just time enough to reach the Haymarket before the scene was discovered, and no change being required in his dress, on the cue being given, Smith appeared 'in his habit as he lived', to the astonishment and mystification of Buckstone—who alone had been carefully kept in ignorance of the matter—and the immense amusement of the whole company assembled at the wings to witness the effect.

'Smith was immediately recognized by the audience, who received him with repeated cheers; and in obedience to a unanimous call, he made his bow to them at the end of the scene, addressing a few pleasant words to them in explanation, and retired amidst hearty laughter and applause both before and behind the curtain.

'In this piece, as in many others, I took the opportunity of promulgating opinions which might be serviceable to the best interests of the Drama. In reply to an observation of *Fortune* (Mrs. Fitzwilliam), the *Spirit of Drury Lane* replied—

"Because of every other hope bereft,
  The Drama is to Fortune's mercy left;
  So much is she your slave, that e'en the weather
  Can ruin all the Theatres together.
  The State no temple to the Drama gives,
  She keeps a shop, and on chance custom lives
  From hand to mouth. What cares she for disgrace,
  While Basinghall Street stares her in the face!
  Will any manager, who's not a ninny,
  To walk the stage, give Roscius one poor guinea,
  When he can double his receipts by dealing
  With a man-fly who walks upon the ceiling!"'

The press was delighted and *The Illustrated London News* said:
'On Monday was inaugurated the new management, with great spirit. Mr. Albert Smith's *Ascent of Mont Blanc* seems to have suggested to Mr. Planché's parodial imagination *Mr. Buckstone's Ascent of Mount Parnassus;* and, accordingly, after the comedy of *The Rivals*, Mr. Buckstone appeared in his character of *Manager*, anxiously enquiring of *Fashion* and *Fortune* (Mr. W. Farren and Mrs. Fitzwilliam) the way to success. Creditably for both, they recommend honest endeavour; and Mr. Buckstone himself confesses to certain poetic aspirations which Mr. C. Marshall has pictorially indulged. The panorama of "the ascent", including a general prospect of Parnassus, and views of the Village of Krissa, the Schiste and the Sacred Way, Ruins of the City of Delphi, the Castalian Fountain, the Corycian Cave, and the Snowy Peak of Liakura, are all admirably and beautifully painted. Of the general hits at things as they are—especially "things theatrical"—we may distinguish the scenes from the *Corsican Brothers*, and the *Gold-diggings*. These were finely painted and humorously accompanied. The dialogue abounds in witty allusions, and, of itself, is an earnest of the promises held out by Mr. Buckstone as to his future management. His predilections in favour of the poetic drama are highly honourable to him, and will, we hope, prove successful.'

Planché also tells that in 1853 he wrote a *lever de rideau* to introduce, on 17 October, Alfred Wigan as manager of the Olympic Theatre. This was to star the 'Great Little Robson' who played the Spirit of Burlesque. Its title, *A Camp at the Olympic*, might be thought to foreshadow the future in another connotation! In the fifties the Volunteer movement had made summer camps and manoeuvres on Wimbledon Common and at Cobham a popular target for satire. *The Illustrated London News* called the piece 'an elegant *revue* of the state of the drama. Tragedy, Comedy, Farce, Opera, Melodrama, and Spectacle, were permitted to urge their respective claims, and maintain an amicable altercation, to the great amusement of the audience. Mr. Planché had, indeed, thrown much wit and humour into the dialogue, which was rendered more interesting by being interpreted by the chief performers of the establishment—Mrs. Chatterly, Mrs. Sterling, Miss Priscilla Horton, Mr. Emery, Mr. Robson, Mr. and Mrs. Wigan and Miss Turner. The war of words concluded with a moral promise, to attempt a new species of drama that should combine the opposite excellencies of those that threatened to become obsolete.'

B

John Buckstone, who is still said to haunt the Haymarket, was to follow his *The Ascent of Mount Parnassus* with other 'Easter Pieces' in the form now becoming established at last. In the next year Planché called his piece 'A New and Original Cosmiographical, Visionary Extravaganza and Dramatic Review,' and took its inspiration from Wyld's Globe, a panorama, then at the height of its popularity, on what is now the garden of Leicester Square.

This 'Trip round the World' at the Haymarket took the opportunity so often resorted to later to 'Bring on the Dancing Girls' as a 'Grand Oriental Spectacle', with 'Miss Lydia Thompson, Miss L. Morris and the *corps de ballet*', while visiting Asia and burlesquing topical events and plays. The playbill ends 'Sic transit gloria (Easter) mundi.'!

The Illustrated London News, 22 April comments:

'The Easter piece that succeeded is, like that of last year, properly a *Revue;* and by means of a diorama, with dramatic accessories, it contrives to make allusion to the public events of the year, and also to connect them arbitrarily with the theatrical business of the season. *Mr. Buckstone's Voyage round the Globe (in Leicester Square)* is the title of this essentially satirical production. The curtain draws up on the exterior of the Haymarket Theatre, where the *Manager* is accosted by an *Author* (Mr. W. Farren), to whom he is indebted for the idea of the piece. Both proceed to the foot of the staircase in Wyld's Model of the Earth, and while seated, in expectation of the lecture, fall asleep, and have a vision of *Cybele* alias *Tellus*, in the person of Mrs. Fitzwilliam. By this Goddess the *Manager* is led to make acquaintance in succession with the tutelar spirits of Europe, Asia, Africa, and America; each of them displaying to his astonished view the most famous scenes in her own quarter of the globe—such as Constantinople and the Golden Horn, Gallipoli, and the theatre of war. But as the managerial dream proceeds, its associations pass from the political to the theatrical, and, as the manner of dreams is, connects together odds and ends of stage-experience, and thus summons before the mind's eye the rival *Richards* of Drury and the Princess's; an Oriental *corps de ballet* in Bayadère costume; the elephant of Astley's; the Feast of the Dragon, and the Chinese feat of impalement, in which the Messrs. Marshall as *Chin Gan* and *Wan Sing*, were singularly successful; the *Aztecs* and Earthmen; gipsies, and Miss Cushman in *Meg Merrilies*, as the first of such weird sisters; the Mexican Sea of Ice at the Adelphi, and "the Struggle for Gold", at all the theatres in the contest for which the stage sinks, and Mr. Buckstone finds himself again in Leicester Square, waked up from his daydreams. The elegance of the dialogue, as usual with Mr. Planché, is the main charm of the piece; and the honourable determination, throughout expressed on the part of the manager, to maintain, at all hazards, the literary character of his theatre, must challenge the regard of the intelligent critic. The performance was warmly received, and the applause at the end such as to raise hopes of its having more than ordinary success.'

Later the same journal, when publishing a picture of the Oriental scene, says:

'Mr. Planché's "Revue" and Mr. Buckstone's *Voyage* meet, we are happy to find, with the success fairly earned by the elegance of the composition and the costly style in which the pictorial and scenic accessories are placed on the boards. The mind is carried through the events of the year by a series of significant symbols, skilfully chosen, and accompanied by remarks in the dialogue—not only witty but wise, calculated to instruct as well as amuse.'

The following Easter Monday Buckstone produced yet a third 'New and Original Extravaganza' *The New Haymarket Spring Meeting 1855*. This appears to have been even more theatrical and parochial than its predecessors.

The Theatrical Journal, 18 April 1855 says:

'Haymarket.—The new piece has proved quite successful. The curtain rises on a view of the interior of Guildhall, in which the City of London (Miss Caroline White) is domiciled. The Lord Mayor's Fool, (Mr. Buckstone), shows to her through an aperture in the scene, the 9th of November. Westminster, (Miss Harriett Gordon), calls on her Easter friend, and a conversation ensues, which chiefly turns on the inexhaustable subject of City improvements. After a little bickering the two cities become excellent friends, and Westminster asking to see the theatres is taken a little beyond the strict London boundary, and introduced to the Standard, the City of London, the Britannia, and the Grecian Saloon, each of which has an allegorical representative. Westminster, in return for this intellectual treat, takes London to the "Ups and Downs," to witness a race for public favour. In front of a very beautiful scene a number of jockeys appear, each leading some celebrity of the day, political or dramatic; thus we have Sebastopol, Balaklava, Louis XI, Janet Pride, Mont Blanc, &c., who with their jockeys, join in a dance, and at last start for the race. How the contest is decided does not appear, for the decoration suddenly changes to a glittering "last scene", in which some *femmes volantes* are introduced, and an address is spoken by Mr. Buckstone. In the art of decorating the stage, Mr. Buckstone shows himself as much a proficient as ever. The dresses are all clear and bright, the scenery is well painted.'

The Illustrated London News, 14 April comments:

'Here there is no faëry tale, but a sporting chronicle, in which "the fancy" claims unwonted license, partly allegorical and partly dramatic. In great part, however, the piece retains the usual character of Mr. Buckstone's Easter entertainments—that of a *revue* of theatrical doings, past, present, and to come.'

Planché in his first reference to Revue notes one solitary exception of which he was not the author. This would, at first glance, seem to be *1863; or, the Sensations of the Past Season with a Shameful Revelation of 'Lady Somebody's Secret,'* by Henry J. Byron, called on the programme 'a comical conglomerative absurdity'. It was produced on Boxing Day to inaugurate the short-lived management of Benjamin Webster at the St. James's Theatre.

The Illustrated London News reviewed the piece on 2 January:

'Mr. Webster having become manager of this theatre, and imported into it some of his Adelphi company, this appears to be the fitting place in the series for a notice of the entertainment at this house. It is *A Revue of Eighteen Hundred and Sixty-three; or, the Sensations of the Past Season, with a Shameful Revelation of Lady Somebody's Secret*. Miss Fanny Josephs represents a modern author, who consults his domestic, Mrs. Brown (Mr. Toole), on the theme for a Christmas piece. Mrs. Brown, who is the loquacious dame lately invented by Mr. Arthur Sketchley, makes a number of impracticable suggestions, when Fancy proposes a *revue* of recent events, ghosts in connection with which pass over the stage. The Haunted Man, Banquo, Hamlet's father, Fabian dei Franchi, and others, however, plead in vain. We have next a hoarding in London, exhibiting all manner of advertisements of playhouses and periodicals, where Fancy introduces Mr. Toole, who parodies Fechter, an actress of Leah, and an actor of Manfred. Miss Josephs herself then represents Robert Audley, and, with George Tallboys (Mr. Paul Bedford), visits Audley Court, when the stage divides, the Gothic Chamber and the Limewalk occupying the two portions; and Mr Toole appears as Lady Audley, and Mr. W. Chamberlain as Sir Michael. Tallboys's immersion in the well forms the great effect of the scene; but a song by Fancy was too long, and provoked some disapprobation. The following scenes, however, restored the audience to good humour: The Land of Thistles, Land of Shamrocks, and the Land of Roses. A tableau of the Prince and Princess of Wales brought down the curtain with great applause. The piece bears on it marks of haste. Mr. Webster appeared at the conclusion, and apologised for the shortness of time in which he had to prepare the performance, the theatre not having come into his possession until the previous Saturday.'

Fanny Josephs was famous for her male impersonations in burlesque and with Toole's several appearances in 'drag' the revue was in the best of later traditions. That this is the exception referred to by Planché is suggested by an American writer, J. Brander Matthews in *The Theatre of Paris*, (1880) when he says:

'These minor Parisian theatres [Folies-Marigny; Bouffes-Parisiens and Variétés] have one peculiarity. On or about the first of January they often produce a piece chronicling and satirising the events of the past year, and obviously called a "review" (*revue*) of the year. Mr. John Brougham endeavoured to naturalize the review in New York when he opened his pretty little Fifth Avenue Theatre in 1869, but the attempt failed. A like result seems to have attended the several attempts of Mr. J. R. Planché, and the single attempt of Mr. H. J. Byron to carry the review across the Channel to England. Novelty of incident is necessary to cloak the similarity of plot. The opportunity the review offers for "local hits" and personalities is too tempting to be missed; but it has been so frequently abused, that, like the custom of producing pantomimes at Christmas in London, the practice of preparing a New Year's annual in Paris began slowly to die out about a decade ago. Within the past two or three years the fashion seems to be coming a little more into favor again.'

It is also possible that Planché may have been referring to another Haymarket regular playwright, Joseph Stirling Coyne, who provided Buckstone with his 'Easter Piece' for 1863, *Buckstone at Home; or, the Manager and his Friends* labelled 'An original domestic and dramatic apropos sketch'. It takes the form more of an inquest on the general state of the drama as well as including individual satire.

The Era, 12 April 1863, says:

'Great consternation is then created amongst the ancient characters by the announcement that Burlesque ("That Graceless Girl") is coming in, for they have all denounced that wicked female as having been the cause of their decadence, Sir Peter Teazle especially saying that in his day the wit of the Stage was like a polished rapier. A person was delicately run through with it, whereas now-a-days he was knocked down with a sledge-hammer joke.

'Burlesque, in the person of Miss Louise Keeley, dances in and embraces the Widow Green as her mother, the widow for that purpose, we presume, being considered the embodiment of high comedy. Burlesque then sings a song, for the

[12]

purpose of introducing the leading burlesque characters of late years; and finally the British Lion is brought on by Britannia [played by none other than a young Ellen Terry] who suggests that the best novelty and the most appropriate one will be a Panorama, and so after this fashion the object of the *apropos* sketch is served.'

Among the characters brought on by Burlesque and condemned by the older generation are creations of both Planché and Byron among others, which may well have annoyed the elder playwright.

The Era comments:

'The present piece is very similar to the burlesque produced at the same house a few years ago, called *The New Haymarket Spring Meeting*, and written by Planché, in which all the burlesques of the day were introduced. There is, however, nothing new under the sun, and if ancient comedy has now to inscribe *Ichabod* on its banners, *Réchauffée* may be a fitting inscription for burlesque.'

The first attempt by John Brougham to stage revue in New York, referred to by Brander Matthews, was for the opening of Brougham's Theatre on 25 January 1869, for which he wrote and staged an after-piece, *The Dramatic Review for 1868*, which was 'No less than a burlesque upon several of the most popular dramas of the present season produced at the different theatres of this City,' (*The Era* 'American Theatricals,' 21 February 1869). It was not a success and, though revised, did not remain in the bill for long.

Brougham, a London actor who had been with Vestris and Mathews at both the Olympic and Covent Garden, made two attempts to found a theatre with his name in New York, both of which failed, though he himself was a successful actor and playwright on both sides of the Atlantic.

It would seem that New York was not yet ready for revue. Opera bouffe and burlesque, particularly with Lydia Thompson and her English company, were the big attraction of the day in this field of light entertainment. London playgoers were in much the same frame of mind and there seems no trace after 1863 of a return to revue for the next thirty years.

AN ABORTIVE START

By the beginning of the nineties taste was rapidly changing in all aspects of the drama and entertainment. Since the last Revue experiments, extravaganzas, burlesques and travesties had completely lost favour, despite an attempted resuscitation. W. Davenport Adams, though he never mentions revue in his excellent *Book of Burlesque* (1891) says:

'With the year 1885 there dawned a new epoch for stage travestie in England. The old Gaiety company had broken up, Miss Farren alone remaining; and with the accession of fresh blood there came fresh methods. The manager [George Edwardes] who had succeeded Mr. Hollingshead recognised the tendencies of the times; and with *Little Jack Sheppard*—a travestie by Messrs. Stephens and Yardley of the well-known story, familiar both in fiction and in drama, novel departure was made.

'In the "palmy" days, burlesque had not, as a rule, formed the whole of an evening's entertainment. The one-act travestie had grown on occasion into two and even three acts; but, until recent years, the one act (in several scenes) had usually been deemed sufficient, the remainder of the programme being devoted to comedy or drama. The musical part of the performance had generally been made up of adaptations or reproductions of popular airs of the day—either comic songs or operatic melodies: very rarely had the music been particularly remarkable; nor, save during the various *régimes* of Vestris, had there been any special splendour in the dresses. For the most part, the old school of burlesque did not rely upon a brilliant *mise-en-scène*.

'A very different policy was to characterise the New Burlesque. The pieces, having now become the staple of the night's amusement, were to be placed upon the boards with all possible splendour. Money was to be spent lavishly on scenery, properties and costumes. Dancing was to be a prominent feature—not the good old-fashioned "breakdowns" and the like, but choreographic interludes of real grace and ingenuity. The music was to be written specially for the productions, and pains were to be taken to secure artists who could really sing.'

The 'New Burlesque' was, however, to be short-lived. Meantime travesties or parodies of current productions continued to be produced at the smaller theatres, mainly at Toole's where the older traditions were carried on till the mid-nineties.

The changes in taste had been dictated by the entertainment-seeking public itself. With the advent of the dull, sanctimonious and hypocritical sixties, when burlesque with its 'naughty' ladies in tights with dubious reputations was not considered family entertainment. Comic opera, opera bouffe or operetta being of continental origin also fell under the displeasure of the more puritan public until Gilbert and Sullivan began to make it respectable once again. At the Empire and the Alhambra comic opera and ballet had held sway and Music Halls were still a lower-class entertainment frequented by the Bohemian literary and sporting fraternity. The Halls did not emerge from this aura until the turn of the century, although their great stars had been acceptable to the middle-class morality in pantomime at Christmas for nearly twenty years.

There had arisen a vast number of popular 'Polite' entertainments and entertainers: the German Reeds, the Howard Pauls (both respectably married couples), George Grossmith senior (at the piano) and many others, who did not perform in actual theatres. There were also the Minstrels in various forms who settled in concert halls in and around London. Early in the nineties the Pierrots or Concert Parties became the stock seaside holiday entertainment and were eventually to find their way to the metropolis for off-season visits.

All these miscellaneous entertainments were less 'parochial' or 'parish pump' than early revue had been, but were to add their quota to the resultant entertainment.

Before this was to happen the 'New Burlesque' had to come and go. George Edwardes, always adventurous, had lost faith in burlesque and was successfully experimenting with musical comedy. From the time of *In Town* at the Prince of Wales' in 1892, the first of the species, it bred quickly.

Strangely enough just over a year later revue again made a reappearance, this time at the Royal Court Theatre where, on 25 November 1893, was produced *Under the Clock*, calling itself an extravaganza on the programme, the work of the actor-authors Seymour Hicks and Charles Brookfield with original music by Edward Jones.

In his reminiscences *Me and my Missus* (1939) Hicks says:

'I asked Charles Brookfield, who was a member of the Court company at the time, if he would write a musical play with me on the lines of a Paris *revue*, but instead of satirizing general topics of interest make the travesty nearly wholly theatrical. This idea he fell in with, and together we wrote what was a most impertinent, and at times rather cruel, burlesque, called "Under the Clock", which was immediately accepted by Mr. Chudleigh and proved phenomenally successful. It was the first revue ever produced in England.

'Brookfield appeared as Sherlock Holmes, and I played his slave of the novel, Dr. Watson. We were supposed to be showing Emile Zola, who at that time was on a visit to London, round the various theatres. Brookfield and myself gave imitations of Henry Irving, Wilson Barrett, Beerbohm Tree, Lady Bancroft, Rose Leclercq, and no end of well-known people, slashing mercilessly at them in a way I should not dream of doing today. For instance, Brookfield made an entrance as Beerbohm Tree in "Hamlet", saying:

> "I'm dressed in black because I did not go;
> These are my trappings and my suits of woe."

And lines put into the mouth of Miss Lottie Venne in her impersonation of a famous and beautiful though somewhat mannered actress [Mrs. Patrick Campbell] were:

> "We modern girls, who don't know how to speak,
> Resort to giving imitation weak
> Of Ellen, who the gift of God inherits;
> Her faults become her pupils' only merits."

'Augustin Daly's company were in London at this time, playing Shakespeare at Daly's Theatre with a wonderful American accent, and I shall never forget the laugh that went up when I entered, dressed in armour, as Richard Coeur de Lion, and said with an American twang: "I am Richard, King of England, and don't you forget it!"

'I possess a letter written by Lady Bancroft to Brookfield expressing her delight with the production, and ending with "What a bundle of talent Hicks is! I see another Robson coming". For many years I thought her ladyship meant I was likely to be another Robson. I now can only suppose that she must have been looking out of her window and caught sight of someone who reminded her of that great little comedian walking towards her house in Berkeley Square.

'In this piece for the first time I sang and danced, and in doing so my whole career became altered. I had supposed that the very legitimate drama was my goal; and singing and dancing as the branch of work I was to stay in for many years never entered my head.'

Hicks seemed unaware of the earlier attempts of Planché and his followers.

The title *Under the Clock* was drawn from the fact that theatrical entertainments were advertised in *The Times* each day with, at the head of the column, the famous wood-cut of the clock face and books.

The revue was the last part of a triple bill which included a one act play by Hicks, *Good-Bye*, and a comedy opera, also in one act, *A Venetian Singer*.

The Era, 2 December 1893, says:

'The sting of the entertainment was in its "tail". The intention of the authors was evidently to imitate the French *revue*. They have confined themselves, however, to a passing survey of a very small section of the events of the year, and their humour is not always of the most good natured sort. In the case of the satire on Mr. Daly's company, it was impossible not to feel that the attack was a trifle inhospitable. Mr. Beerbohm Tree can afford to be amused at raillery which only testifies to his fame; but there seems to be a want of kindliness in the ridicule cast upon the American accent and other peculiarities of our visitors from across the Atlantic. The piece opens in the study of Sherlock Holmes, Mr. Conan Doyle's marvellously clever detective, who is waited on by Dr. Watson, and visited by M. "Emile Nana". There is a good deal of fun poked at Holmes, and we get to the Mansion House, where there is a chorus of foresters from Tennyson's play. Here the variety entertainment came in, and the efforts of the artists "saved the show". Mr. Seymour Hicks was indefatigable. He assumed the garb of Coeur de Lion, and mimicked the Yankee accent. He and Mr. Brookfield stood behind a row of headless portraits painted on a canvas screen, and, placing their faces in the proper positions, imitated various well-known actors and actresses. But the cleverest imitations of all were done by Miss Lottie Venne. It was worth passing some rather tame quarters of an hour to see and hear Miss Venne, as with marvellous acuteness and exquisite humour she caricatured Mrs. Patrick Campbell's Paula and "took off" Miss Rose Leclercq and Miss Julia Neilson. There was more than mere mimicry, there was keen and racy humour in this. Miss Venne knows by a subtle instinct exactly how far to go in the direction of exaggeration, and her drollery is delicately fine. Mr. Brookfield, got up as Mr. Beerbohm Tree in *The Tempter*, was perched on the capital of a pillar, and recited some lines which smartly burlesqued Mr. H. A. Jones's hyper-Elizabethan verbiage in that play. This was decidedly the most intelligent and literary part of the "book" of *Under the Clock*, in which, however, there are a good many smart lines. Less humorous, because more bluntly personal, was the introduction of four personages representing Mr. Tree in as many of his favourite characters, the quartette joining in a chorus ridiculing the actor's versatility. If to be versatile be a crime, many an artist we wot of is entirely free from condemnation. Such "adaptable" workers as Mr. Brookfield and Mr. Hicks should be the last to deride versatility. *Under the Clock* is not exactly an instance of exquisite humour; but, with such able artists in the cast, there should be no difficulty in "working up" the piece into a success by the simple but always effective process of cutting out all that does not "go", and adding new and amusing matter. Of Miss Lottie Venne we have already written. Not only were her imitations immensely successful; her deft handling of some lively ditties won encores. Mr. Brookfield and Mr. Hicks worked hard, and kept things moving by their able exertions. Mr. Robert Nainby made quite a little hit as "Emile Nana", his share in a *can-can* being both active and amusing. Mr. Wyes made a properly ponderous Master of the Ceremonies; Miss Maude Wilmot tripped and posed with grace and activity; and, with a pair of other ladies, did some neat dances arranged by Madame Marriette D'Auban. The dresses supplied by L. and H. Nathan were effective, and Mr. T. W. Hall's scenery was just what was required. There was some sibilation towards the end of *Under the Clock*, but the authors were called at the conclusion, when few, if any, dissentient voices were heard.'

In the notice by the critic of *The Theatre* (1 January 1894) we see the founda-
tions of the very thing which was eventually to help kill intimate Revue in our
time for both the general public and the critics, and can only be described as its
theatrical bitchiness!:

'For this burlesque, *revue*, extravaganza, or what not, London has been
thirsting for weeks. And now that London has it, I am not sure that London will
know how to take it. Mr. Brookfield has a pretty wit to look at, but the sting of
a scorpion lies in its tail, and this sting he has here brought overmuch into play.
It is announced that every care has been taken to avoid hurting anyone's feelings
in the course of the satire. But if this be the authors' view, their feelings must be
as hard to hurt as a rhinoceros, for merciless are the lashings they "carefully"
inflict upon their unhappy victims.

'Burlesque of this kind has never been divorced from a certain geniality in
tone. Harmless foibles have been exaggerated to awaken good-natured laughter.
Mr. Toole for instance has put on a Roman nose, struck ridiculous pseudo-
classic attitudes, and called himself Wilson Barrett. "Adonis" Dixey has represented Mr. Irving as *Hamlet* pumping water from a well. Miss Eastlake's crow's
nest *coif*, her jerky ways and emotional explosions were comically magnified by
Miss Marie and Miss Laura Linden. And even in Mr. Brookfield's *Poet and
Puppets* at the Comedy, scarce more than legitimate chaff was levelled at the
"foolishly fertile" Mr. Wilde. But at the Court it is quite another matter. True
the jester's sounding bladder is not discarded altogether; but as often as not it is
vitriol that is used, and the very bitterness of the attack defeats the object in view.
What does the public know or care about the tiffs and enmities, the envy and the
spleen of actors!'

Both Hicks, then aged only twenty-two, and Brookfield, thirty-six, were
already noted as actors and writers and for their witticisms and biting satire,
particularly the latter, whose barbed sallies, both in his plays and in real life were
much quoted. He became the Examiner of Plays in 1911 and was ever ready in
this new capacity as Censor to clamp down with a firm hand on any sign of
liberality, particularly in what had been his own particular province!

Hicks was snapped up by Edwardes hoping to save the fast-dying burlesque at the Gaiety in 1894, when he became immediately involved in the
first fully fledged musical comedy there, *The Shop Girl*. Soon followed to the
Gaiety by his wife, Ellaline Terriss, he and she formed a partnership famous in
musical comedy.

For the next few years musical managements were so busy with the new
found money maker that revue once again drifted into the background[1]. At the
turn of the century two authors, who had made their names under George
Edwarde's banner, joined to write *Pot-Pourri*, which was tried out on tour. It
came, labelled an Easter Review (history repeating itself!), to the Coronet
Theatre at Notting Hill Gate in April 1899 and to the Avenue Theatre on 9 June.

The Era, 17 June 1899 says:

'*Pot-Pourri*. A "Revue" of 1899, in Two Parts and Eight Scenes. Written by
James T. Tanner, Lyrics by W. H. Risque, Music by Napoleon Lambelet.

'There is of necessity a risk in trying upon the play-going public a novel form
of entertainment, not new, be it said, in the sense that it has never been done
before, but at any rate unfamiliar in this country to the large majority of theatre-

goers. Paris is the home of the *revue*, and Paris fashions, theatrical and otherwise, are not always popular in London. But there seems no reason why a musical piece of the pattern of *Pot-Pourri* should not find ready acceptance on this side of the English Channel. It has some strong recommendations to favour. The charm of comparative novelty is not to be overlooked; and in this humorous review of recent events the very latest can be made the subject of witty comment; or if someone becomes suddenly conspicuous, his counterfeit presentment can be introduced without much difficulty. The large and representative audience assembled at the Avenue on the opening night were unanimous in their approval of the new piece, the verdict being that it fulfilled all the conditions of a bright and attractive entertainment. Mr. James Tanner has displayed considerable ingenuity in devising a story that readily lends itself to the introduction of numerous characters and up-to-date items. Lord Algy is one of the most important personages in the piece and it is on his wedding-day that the Great Ruby is stolen by thieves and placed inside the bride cake. This is carried off by De Renskey, a street-singer disguised as a broken-down tenor, who abducts Edna, the Belle of New York, to Trafalgar Square, where he hands the cake to a sandwich man. All the time the ruby is safe in the care of Jane, Edna's smart maid, who has taken it out of the cake before the latter was removed by De Renskey. In the Trafalgar Square scene Nelson comes down from his column and sings a song, and then the two thieves and De Renskey, in pursuit of the ruby, get to Saffron Hill, and sing a popularly sentimental trio amongst the organ-grinders there. Henley, at regatta time, is the next scene, and here the ruby is placed by Rosa in the car of a balloon, in which Lord Algy, now transformed to the Rev. Gavin Dishart, in *The Little Minister*, ascends with Edna in triumph. In their transit to France, his lordship, ignorant of the value of the contents of the cigarette-box in which Jane has packed the jewel, throws it into the sea. The three thieves at once form a Submarine Syndicate to fish for it, and in the third scene of the second act we have a "skit" on the diving business in *The White Heather*. Algy recovers the ruby: the rogues are baffled; and all ends happily.

'All the principals work exceedingly hard. The frequent change of dress and make-up is in itself a severe tax upon them, but they "get through" with remarkable energy and spirit. Mr. Farren Soutar does wonders: and his imitations of prominent actors are very clever. His gallery of portraits includes Mr. C. H. Hawtrey, Earl of Poulett, Mr. Pinero, Mr. Cyril Maude as the Little Minister, Mr. Hayden Coffin, Mr. Charles Wyndham, Sir Thomas Lipton, Mr. Tree as D'Artagnan. Specially laughable were Mr. Soutar's imitations of Mr. Coffin and Mr. Wyndham, who is represented in the act of mopping up the tears which flow so copiously during the representation of Mr. Haddon Chambers's play. Mr. E. Dagnall as Hugh S. A. De Wint, the millionaire theatrical manager, appears in the guise of Drivelli, from *The Circus Girl*, and afterwards gives a realistic rendering of Mr. Lowenfeld; appearing later as Mr. H. A. Jones. Mr. Robert Nainby as Legge, a photographer, makes up as Arthur Roberts in the part of Gentleman Joe, and in the course of the evening supplies capital portraits of Zola, Sardou, and the gallant musketeer Athos. Porthos has a capital exponent in Mr. Stephen Adeson, who also scores with his highly amusing portrait of Mr. Gilbert Hare, in *The Gay Lord Quex*. He, however, is not so successful in his imitation of Sir Harry Irving as Robespierre, though his Dreyfus is not at all bad.

Mr. Charles Goodhart as Sir George R. Dagonet neatly hits off the well-known dramatist and journalist, and satirical allusions to a certain hair restorer are, of course, freely introduced. Mr. Goodhart is also seen as the redoubtable W. G. Grace, ready to face the most deadly bowling of the Australian team. Mr. John Le Hay as De Renskey is an important contributor to the fun and frolic. Besides depicting such opposite characters as Aramis, Paderewski, and Mr. John Hare as the Gay Lord Quex, he introduces his well-known ventriloquial entertainment with much success, the familiar figure of the old man with the cotton gloves being dressed to represent a dummy military chairman of a company meeting. Miss Claire Romaine as Jane, the lady's maid, quite appreciates the spirit of the burlesque and faithfully carries out the intention of the author. Her impersonations include a Cockney newsboy, Little Miss Nobody; Miss Maud Millett, in *The Tyranny of Tears;* Biggs, from *The Circus Girl;* Miss Fortescue, in the Globe play; La Poupée, and Jaggers. As a paper boy she sings a capital song in brisk style, but her biggest hit of all is made with the ditty "Mary was a housemaid", with a haunting "bouche fermée" refrain. She sings the song admirably, and on Friday evening was recalled several times. Miss Marie Dainton, a clever recruit from the variety halls, appears as Edna, and amongst her numerous disguises may be mentioned the Runaway Girl, Lady Babbie, Miss Marie Tempest, Miss Mary Moore in the Criterion piece, and Miss Irene Vanbrugh. Very refined and delicate are Miss Dainton's methods, and her success was complete and unequivocal. Her imitations of Miss Letty Lind, and other stage favourites evoked on Friday some of the loudest applause heard during the evening. Mdlle. Jane May gives a remarkably clever imitation of Yvette Guilbert, but is even more successful in a burlesque of Sarah Bernhardt's Hamlet, the tones of voice and manner of the French tragedienne being imitated with striking exactness. Favourable mention must also be made of Miss Susie Nainby's graceful and coquettish French dancing girl, while praiseworthy work was done by Mr. Frank Collins as Arthur Drury, of the Lane, and Mr. Claude Calthorpe as the Spirit of Shakespeare. Mr. Harry Fairleigh as the Statue of Nelson sings a patriotic song with good effect. The chorus deserves favourable mention, the dresses are in excellent taste, and a word of praise is due to Mr. Parker's stage-management.

'An incident, which at first somewhat startled the audience, was the sudden interruption of a venerable-looking gentleman, attired as a bishop, who from a stage box addressed Mr. Pinero's representative on the stage with regard to his much discussed play *The Gay Lord Quex*, but the dignitary of the church showed a surprising readiness to accept an invitation to come behind the scenes, and quickly disappeared amidst the laughter of the audience, who seemed to fully appreciate the joke. At the conclusion of the performance the author, Mr. Jas. T. Tanner, the leading members of the company, and the new managers of the theatre, Messrs. Morell and Mouillot, were called before the curtain, amidst a scene of great enthusiasm.'

Neither this production nor *Under the Clock*, though successful, had long runs and once again the attempts to establish revue proved abortive, though a strange hybrid called *A Dream of Whitaker's Almanack*, 'An up-to-date review of Fun, Fact and Fancy', was produced in June (two days before *Pot-Pourri* opened) at the Crystal Palace Theatre, but was not heard of again.

The Linkman; or, Gaiety Memories, in two scenes, by George Grossmith Junior was, what Planché would have called, a *pièce de circonstance*, being written as part of a programme for the final months of the old Gaiety Theatre in 1903, also under this heading comes a revue *Shakespeare v Shaw*, especially written by J. B. Fagan for a benefit matinée for the actor, H. B. Conway, at the Haymarket Theatre on 18 May 1905. Though called 'A Revue' on the programme it had no music, and seems to have been more of a one-act satire, in which it was alleged that Shaw (Edmund Maurice) was charged that 'he had libelled Shakespeare [Cyril Maude] by the statement that he wrote plays just as good and other similarly disparaging remarks'; various stars were called to bear witness and as always on these occasions 'a good time was had by all!'

ESTABLISHED AT LAST

With the turn of the century, the death of the old Queen, and the emergence of Edwardian society from its Victorian cocoon, the atmosphere of the *entente cordiale* created by King Edward provided a fertile soil in which to re-sow the seeds of French revue, which itself had been enjoying a notable revival across the Channel.

The music halls, as the Victorian masses knew them, were fast becoming palaces of variety and setting out to attract family audiences. The London Coliseum opened in 1904, the Lyceum was re-built as a music hall the same year, the London Hippodrome, first a circus in 1900, gave way to variety in 1909, the Empire and the Alhambra were still strongholds of ballet interspersed with variety, and the Palace, opened as the Royal English Opera House in 1891, became the Palace Theatre of Varieties in 1892 and was setting out to attract stars from the theatre, musical comedy and ballet by the early years of the century. In fact real music hall was virtually killing itself with refinement, and when 'The Cinderella of the Arts at last went to the Ball' with the Royal Command performance of 1912, the decline had well set in, and revue, which this time had been engendered within its own walls, began its ivylike process of extermination.

It must be remembered that the music halls had come under the jurisdiction not of the Lord Chamberlain but of the L.C.C. and Licensing Magistrates (for music, singing and dancing only), and dialogue in play form was not allowed. If sketches were tried by adventurous music hall managers the full rigour of the Law was often invoked.

In June 1904 the following statement with respect to the 'sketch question' was published on behalf of the Theatrical Managers' Association:

'Many inaccurate statements have been circulated with regard to the position taken up by theatrical managers towards music hall sketches. These statements have created a considerable misapprehension in the public mind, and the theatrical managers of the United Kingdom consider that the time has come to clearly define their position. Theatres have been for the last sixty years, and still are, regulated under the Stage Play Act, passed in 1843. The Act provides for the licensing of theatres and the censorship by the Lord Chamberlain of all performances taking place therein. Its provisions have been rightly enforced by the authorities, and theatre licences are granted and renewed under its powers every year. Music halls are licensed under an older Act, which does not impose any censorship or restrictions upon the performances to be given; but at the same time it does not in any way sanction the performance of stage plays. In course of time there has arisen a practice of presenting at music halls, in addition to the variety entertainment consisting of songs, dances, and other performances, slight sketches, with two or three performers, and lasting about a quarter of an hour. Attempts have been made from time to time in past years by the music halls to extend such performances, but these encroachments have frequently been met by proceedings under the above Stage Play Act. During recent years, these sketches have gradually grown into plays; but so long as they did not form the principal part of the evening's entertainment, and did not constitute too serious a breach of the law, no action was taken by the managers, and it might fairly have been expected that music hall proprietors would have appreciated this spirit of tolerance. Instead of this, they have taken advantage of the licence thus given gradually to increase the length, the importance, and the dramatic interest of these sketches, until at the present time most of the music halls, and particularly those in the suburbs and provinces, take upon themselves to present complete dramatic pieces, with unlimited characters, numerous scenes, and occupying as much time as the particular proprietor thinks desirable.

'It is claimed by theatrical managers that the theatre and the music hall are separate institutions, with separate regulations and privileges. The music halls are permitted to have smoking and drinking in the auditorium, and standing in the corridors; their performances are not subjected to censorship; they are, moreover, permitted in many instances to have what are called "promenades," and in other ways, they enjoy those free and easy attributes which have become associated with the music hall. The privilege of presenting stage plays, hitherto enjoyed by the theatre, is now claimed as a right by the music halls, without their being subjected to the stringent regulations which control the theatre. This condition of things is described as "equality" and "free trade in amusements"! It seems scarcely in accordance with the rights of man that any class of the community should claim that, by breaking a law sufficiently often, they can make a law unto themselves.

'The Theatrical Managers' Association have endeavoured to negotiate an amicable agreement as to the limit of such sketches, and various attempts have been made to arrive at an understanding with a view to rendering further proceedings unnecessary. The theatre managers in the first instance suggested that sketches should be confined to four speaking parts and six supers, with one scene, and a time limit of twenty to twenty-five minutes. This, it is asserted, is all that is required for a sketch in a variety entertainment. These terms were declined. Subsequently the theatre managers increased their offer to six speaking parts and twelve supers, with a time limit of thirty minutes. These terms were also declined by the music hall proprietors, who, meanwhile, continued the performances of unlimited sketches. All attempt at compromise has so far been on the part of the theatre managers, who always have been, and still are, desirous of arriving at an amicable agreement. But the music hall proprietors have rejected all the proposals made to them, and insist upon being permitted to play stage plays without a licence, practically to such extent as they think proper. Once more, with a view to avoid further proceedings, a general meeting of the theatre managers was recently held, when, notwithstanding the stubborn attitude of the music hall proprietors, it was determined to offer one more compromise, and to abstain from prosecutions if the music hall proprietors would agree to limit their performances to sketches having six principal or speaking parts, sixteen chorus or supernumeraries, with a time limit of thirty minutes certain, and with no limit as to scenes. This was felt to be the utmost concession which theatre managers could make. The offer has been formally made, and, if refused, it can only mean that the music hall proprietors intend to insist upon a continuance of that law-breaking which is deprecated by theatre managers. It is hoped, however, that this suggestion will be held to be one of great liberality, and that the music halls will recognise it as such, and consent to a compromise on these terms. The theatre managers are aware that the music hall proprietors are endeavouring to obtain new legislation with a view to bringing about what is called "free trade in amusements". The managers of theatres are fully prepared for legislation on equitable lines. But if "free trade" is to apply to the music halls it must apply to theatres. For it would be manifestly unfair to give to the music halls the right possessed by the theatre while withholding from the theatre the privileges possessed by the music halls. If the music halls are permitted to perform stage plays, then these stage plays should be subject to the same censorship and restrictions as in the case of the theatre. If there is to be drinking and smoking in the auditorium of music halls, clearly the managers of theatres would have an equal right to claim such a privilege. If there is to be a "promenade" in the music halls, the managers of theatres would have the right, if they so chose, to avail themselves of the financial advantages of such an institution. It is doubtful whether the public desire this state of things, and in any case it is probable that the theatres would prefer to retain their present status. There is an alternative scheme for new legislation. That is, that in no place of public entertainment should drinking and smoking be allowed in the auditorium, that there shall be no promenade, and that all stage plays shall be under a controlling authority.'

At the theatres' instigation a partial agreement and truce was reached by 1907, provided the play did not exceed half an hour, but it was not till 1912 that the long controversy was finally settled and the halls came under the Lord Chamberlain and the wiles of the Censor. This fact was to restrict the early music hall revues mainly to song, dance and mime.

All through the late nineties and the early nineteen-hundreds the work of *The Follies* had been contributing to the foundation of intimate revue. Started as an amateur Pierrot company, it was taken over by one of its members, H. G. Pelissier, in 1897, and had several successful seaside seasons. From the first Pelissier developed burlesque and mime in the true revue tradition.

By 1900 they were in London at the Queen's Hall and from then on they gradually insinuated themselves into the music hall bills at the Tivoli, the Alhambra, the Palace and the Empire with their programmes of songs and burlesques of pantomime, music hall and opera. They had a command performance at Sandringham in 1904 and in 1907 they entered the theatre, appearing at the Royalty for a season and including the first of their famous potted plays. From there they went to Terry's and the Apollo where, from February 1908 until he died in 1913 aged 39, Pélissier and his company were appearing almost continually. Their work was a milestone in the development of intimate revue and, though fundamentally a concert party, they span the transition from music hall to theatrical revue.

The Follies had several imitators even in London itself, though nothing again really succeeded in this vein until *The Co-optimists* appeared in 1921.

With the engagement of *The Follies* as part of music hall bills the managers introduced the worm that was to destroy the apple. The Empire, Leicester Square, had specialised since 1887 in high class variety, with two ballets in a classically popular mould, one in each half of the programme. The various managers, including Augustus Harris and George Edwardes, had maintained a standard which, with Wilhelm as designer and Adeline Genée as ballerina, had been as justly famous the world over as had its notorious promenade!

In 1904 the Empire was closed for alterations and when it re-opened on 9 October 1905 one of the traditional ballets had disappeared, and in its place was 'A Revue, or a Collection of Musical Turns,' called *Rogues and Vagabonds*, written by George Grossmith Jnr., of the Gaiety Theatre. George Edwardes had at last taken an interest in revue.

The new Gaiety Theatre was safely launched with musical comedy, but at Daly's Theatre Edwardes was finding the vein of English musical play running out and French light opera was not filling the gap. It needed the importation of Vienna's *The Merry Widow* in 1907 to put that theatre again on the right road, meantime Edwardes' next Empire revue was *Venus—1906*, but after that he lost interest.

Revue did not come again to the Empire till 1908 with *Oh Indeed!* and from then, on and off, there was usually a topical revue in the bill. *Come Inside* (1909), *Hullo . . . London!* and *Hullo . . . People!* (both in 1910), *By George*, the Coronation revue of 1911, *Everybody's Doing It*, which introduced Irving Berlin's ragtime hit to London in 1912, *All the Winners* (1913), *Nuts and Wine, Merry Go Round, By Jingo If We Do* (all in 1914) and *Watch Your Step* (1915). This year saw the last of the Empire ballets; times had indeed changed. Alfred Butt had taken over in 1914 and in 1916 revue occupied the whole evening, (except for a couple of opening turns which themselves soon vanished) and remained till musical comedy pushed its way into the theatre in 1917.

With the new move once made by Edwardes in 1905 other managers soon copied. Oswald Stoll at the Coliseum staged *The 'Revue'* an unashamed importation from Paris 'invented and produced' by Victor de Cottens from the Chatelet and the Folies Bergère.

The Coliseum was giving four houses each day with two different entertainments, one of which, *The 'Revue'*, occupied the complete 3 o'clock and 9 o'clock performances and a book of the lyrics was given with the programme. Though a success, revue did not become an established part of the Coliseum programmes. All these early 'variety' ventures had a *compère* or *commère* in the true Parisian style. The only revue produced in the legitimate theatre at this time was *Hands Up* by an assortment of authors and composers, given at a charity matinee by members of the Savage Club at Her Majesty's Theatre in June 1907.

It was not till 1912 that the craze for revue really took hold of the public. This obsession can be associated with the advent of the new American ragtime rhythm which began to be heard on the halls. Songs by Irving Berlin like 'Alexander's Rag-time Band,' written 1911, changed the face of popular music and proved immediately to the public's taste; his 'Everybody's Doing It' gave its name to the new revue at the Empire in February 1912. An attempt was made early in December to transfer this revue, coupled with a dramatic playlet, to the Apollo Theatre, the stronghold of *The Follies*, but it was back again at the Empire for Christmas.

At the Alhambra, the other home of variety and ballet, on another side of Leicester Square from the Empire, a new régime under André Charlot and M. V. Leveaux took over, after the old theatre had had one of its many face-lifts, and opened on 14 October 1912 with *Kill That Fly!* a far more spectacular revue than had been seen at the Empire, but still preceded by a variety programme. Charlot was to make his name world famous later with a different style of more intimate revue, and bring this art to New York in the twenties, but in 1912 he was pioneering on a wider scale. At the same time Albert de Courville, who was in charge of the London Hippodrome, had just brought to London the American Rag-time Octette, with Melville Gideon at the piano. Songs like 'Hitchy Koo', 'Robert E. Lee', 'You made me love you', 'Oh you beautiful doll', swept the country on gramophone records and authentic ragtime was heard for the first time in this country.

On 23 December de Courville staged his first great spectacular American revue, *Hullo, Rag-time!* complete with singers like Shirley Kellogg and Ethel Levey and a large dancing chorus to parade the joy plank; and a sketch by James Barrie was included to make a full evening's entertainment. Albert de Courville tells the story of his work, with a disarming disregard for accuracy, in his auto-biography *I Tell You* (1928).

By the beginning of 1913 B. W. Findon, the editor of *The Play Pictorial*, in a number devoted to revue, sums up the new trends:

'Those two famous houses of entertainment, the Empire and the Alhambra, are now providing a class of piece that has been a common feature of Parisian life for many a long year, but which is, strictly speaking, only in its infancy with us, and it will certainly not arrive at maturity until the English people have developed a keener sense of humour, and are quicker to appreciate the winged darts of the modern Aristophanes.

'The humour of our *Revues* is characteristically obvious, and those finer shafts of satire which should give them their most appetising value, would, in all probability, fly high above the heads of those who laugh with their eyes, rather than with their minds.

'We have not yet been educated properly as to the possibilities of politics on the stage. We are Party men. We cannot laugh as good humouredly at a "palpable hit" against our own men and matters as we lustily cheer a "hit" at the expense of our opponents. Why the satirist who writes for the stage should be pinioned, while his brother of *Punch* has freedom to fly the empyrean in search of prey, is one of those things that "no fellah can understand".

'My ideal *Revue* will arrive when people have become thoroughly accustomed to satire on the stage, when they can heartily appreciate a joke levelled at themselves, and when the respective managements keep their tame Aristophanes on the premises, who with ready wit and nimble pen can daily prepare his quip and crank on the news of the day, for the evening's consumption.

'It is, in a great measure, due to Mr. Walter Dickson, the managing director of the Empire, that we owe the present popularity of the *Revue*. It was he who commissioned Mr. George Grossmith to write *Hullo . . . London!* which was followed with *By George*, and subsequently, *Everybody's Doing It*, the broad humours of which have filled the auditorium of the Empire these many months past.

'Of more recent date is *Kill that Fly!* which inaugurated the Leveaux-Charlot *régime* at the newly reconstructed and redecorated Alhambra. The title is somewhat vague, but there is no vagueness in the entertainment or in the success that has attended its production.

'In each of the two pieces that are now attracting the favourable attention of the public there has been a distinct advance in the direction of the *Revue* as it is understood in Paris. At the Alhambra a mild effort has been made to indulge in political satire, and the good-natured skit at the expense of Messrs. Asquith, Lloyd George and McKenna harms nobody and amuses many.

'Mr. George Edwardes is a well known personality "behind the scenes" and on the Turf, but it is doubtful if the Rehearsal Scene makes any definite appeal to the general public.

'A marked feature in connection with the *Revue* is that it has brought to the front a special type of entertainer—the versatile artist who can quickly and effectually identify himself with characters as remote from each other as the upper and nether Poles, and who is at home in every kind of situation.

'It would be a work of supererogation to give any detailed *resumé* of the above mentioned *Revues*, for the simple reason, they are as changeable as the weather. The watchful eye of the manager is ever on the look out to introduce some fresh feature or novel scene: but, as I have remarked above, there is room for more enterprise if the *Revue* is to become the *Punch* of the stage and an entertainment that will engage the attention of the wittiest writers of the day, for the Aristophanes of the theatre should, like the newspaper editor, be ever ready to consider contributions from outside.

'I have little to say about the production at the Hippodrome, for the reason that, although labelled a *Revue*, I do not consider it strictly entitled to be classed as such. The scene with the dramatists is its best claim, but with all due deference to its distinguished author, [J. M. Barrie] it is the dullest piece of dramatic humour that has engaged the attention of his delightful pen. Otherwise, the entertainment is pleasant and genial enough, and well calculated to please the Hippodrome clientèle.'

This is the first mention of political satire and the actual personification of living politicians in revue. W. S. Gilbert, under the pseudonym of F. Tomline, (in collaboration with Gilbert à Beckett) had burlesqued his own play *The Wicked World* as *The Happy Land* at the Royal Court in 1873. In this he had included a grotesque dance by three actors made up as Mr. Gladstone and two members of his Cabinet. This caused the Lord Chamberlain to step in and demand immediate alterations. It would appear that in the few years before the Censor took control of the halls they seem to have taken advantage of the license allowed them which was greater than that granted to the legitimate theatre!

THE ROAD DIVIDES: SPECTACULAR AND INTIMATE

With spectacular revue now established as a popular entertainment in the variety theatres less room remained for satire, either theatrical or political. These

C

revues were built round singers and songs (often transatlantic), exhibition dancers with large choruses of dancing girls and usually a star comedian from the Halls for good measure. The exploitation of the 'hit' song, now mostly ragtime or jazz, passed often from variety to revue, helped largely by the rise in popularity of the gramophone.

This formula had crystallized itself in New York through the genius of Florenz Ziegfeld, who began to 'glorify the American show-girl' in 1907 with a revue built round his star singer Nora Bayes[2]. An exchange of English and American artists, rather than actual shows, was to follow over the next two decades. English artists were also welcome in the similar productions in both Paris and Berlin during the pre-war years.

De Courville, the English Ziegfeld, at the Hippodrome produced *Hullo, Tango!* (1913), *Business as Usual* (1914), *Push and Go* (1915), *Joyland* (1915), *Flying Colours!* (1916), *Zig-Zag!* (1917), *Box o' Tricks!* (1918), *Joy-Bells!* (1919) and *Jig-Saw!* (1920). Titles which themselves almost comment on the drift of events during the Great War. Besides presenting the revues De Courville himself wrote them, mostly in association with Wal Pink, a combination which was also responsible for many touring productions.

At the Alhambra the Charlot régime continued with *8d a Mile* (1913), *Keep Smiling* (1913), *Not Likely!* (1914), *5064 Gerrard* (1915) until broken by *The Bing Boys are Here* in 1916, a strange mixture called revue on the programme but really more a musical comedy.

The Palace, under Alfred Butt, went over to revue in 1914 with *The Red Heads* followed by *The Passing Show* the same year, *Bric-à-Brac* (1915), *Vanity Fair* (1916), *Airs and Graces* (1917), *Hullo, America!* (1918), *The Whirligig* (1919). The Palace revues did go in for satire and topicality and were more consistent productions than those at the other two theatres.

All these revues were a clever compilation under the overall planning of the producer with his own associate writers and composers. Many writers of sketches, lyrics and music were employed as were the famous magazine artists and designers of the day.

At the rebuilt Middlesex Music Hall in Drury Lane Oswald Stoll was indulging in a series of French importations *à la Folies Bergère* with titles full of 'spicy' innuendo. *Cachez Ça!* (1913), *C'Est Chic!* (1913), *C'Est Bon!* (1914), *Vive l'Amour* (1914) are among them. Other large London theatres and music halls throughout the war years staged revues in one form or another, giving a haven for the artists from the fast-vanishing music halls and variety theatres up and down the country, and the kind of entertainment needed in war time.

Touring revue was the temporary salvation of the halls, which had become refined into variety theatre by the time of the Royal Command Performance of 1912. In fact a glance at the cast of this performance shows the infiltration of revue in the inclusion of Ida Crispi and Fred Farren from the Empire's *Everybody's Doing It* (though, because of a last minute quarrel, they did not actually appear).

From 1912 onwards hundreds of specially constructed revues travelled their way up and down the country, playing the twice nightly provincial and suburban dates, their titles sometimes paraphrasing those of successful London productions (*What Ho Ragtime*, *Passing Events*, *Dance This Way*). Some were held together by a general theme, *Grouse and Heather* a Scottish revue, *Monte Carlo to Tokio* a ballet revue, *Way Back to Darkey Land* a minstrel revue, *While You Wait* a wild west revue, all in 1913! A familiar picture which was to continue up to the 1950's when television finally shut down the provincial halls.

In the West End of London the 'Spectacular' into which it eventually developed, and which survives to this day at the London Palladium, was challenged by a new form from Paris introduced into London by C. B. Cochran in October 1914. To say challenged may be a misstatement as 'intimate' revue was aimed at a sophisticated theatre-going public, as opposed to the popular variety-music hall audience now successfully catered for by the spectacular revue. It was to make a sharp division of the term 'Revue' into two distinct forms, and it is on the intimate style that the main interest of the next forty years centres.

Spectacular revue from the early days shared many famous names from variety and musical comedy like George Robey, Violet Loraine, Nelson Keys, Elsie Janis and Gertie Millar, and often introduced 'Speciality Acts' entirely divorced form the main production. The Original Dixieland Jazz Band was heard in *Joy-Bells!* (1919) and Paul Whiteman and his Orchestra in *Brighter London* (1923), both at the London Hippodrome.

The new intimate style was especially designed to exploit a particular talent or talents.

C. B. Cochran, the great impresario, in *Secrets of a Showman* (1925) says:

'I had long visualised for London a revue on the lines of those at the Capucines and other small theatres in Paris. The new Ambassadors Theatre in the Seven Dials seemed ideal for the purpose. After the acquisition of the lease, or, to be technically correct, a three years' agreement, I began to look for talent.

'At the Olympia, Paris, where I had gone to see a star dancer, I noticed, playing a part of some half a dozen lines, a young woman, who appeared to me to be possessed of a curious magnetism. Her only chance was in a burlesque of a current play by Henri Bataille. She was impersonating Yvonne de Bray in one of her emotional moments. This young woman had the "tear in the voice". That gift cannot be acquired. But you can sit with your eyes shut in any theatre and know that you are listening to a big artist directly the voice gives you a tremor down the spine.

' "Who is this girl?" I said to Adolph Braff, the variety agent, who was with me. "You must know her," he replied. "She was several years in London, where you must have met her as Madame Harry Fragson. She parted from Fragson a year before his tragic murder by his father, and went back to the stage to make a living. They call her Alice Delysia."

'I did, indeed, remember having met the young woman in London. One night in Fragson's flat she kept a party of us entranced with her simple singing of a number of old French ballads. I said to her then: "Why don't you go on the stage?" Fragson retorted: "She would drive everybody out of the theatre!" And I remember, too, that she said she would be no good in the theatre; she had tried it and had not got beyond the chorus.

'That night in Paris I met John Tiller, famous all over the world for his English dancers. I asked him if he knew Delysia, and he told me that as a chorus girl she was full of promise. Always she had been ready to deputise for anybody who was "off", from Mistinguett to Marnac, and always she gave a good account of herself. "But," added Tiller, "the French manager seldom recognises an artist till she is forty years of age."

'Shortly after this I saw Delysia deputising for Mrs. Vernon Castle, who was making her first success in Paris. Delysia was not a dancer, but her natural sense of the stage enabled her to give a most creditable performance. I did not engage Delysia at our first meeting, because she was tied up by a contract that contained several options, but she promised that when she could get free she would come to London.

'I got possession of the Ambassadors Theatre in August 1914, and that determined me to devote my energies to theatre management. I had made a number of engagements and had a revue in the making, but my original arrangements were destined to non-fulfilment by reason of the Great War. For the first month or two it was doubtful if the theatres would remain open. In October I decided to make a start, but with a revue applicable to the times and with a cosmopolitan cast, which I felt would appeal to the many strangers within our midst. I engaged Max Dearly and Jeanne St. Bonnet; Leon Morton, the attenuated droll, who had often amused me in Paris; and Delysia, who by now had come to London. The principal English players were J. M. Campbell; Millie Sim, the charming daughter of Millie Hylton, who is now Mrs. Stanley Mills; little Betty Balfour, now the film star; and several other useful people. I particularly wanted eight English dancing girls, the Grecian Maids, who, under the direction of J. W. Jackson, had been a feature of Reinhardt's Munich production of *La Belle Hélène;* but they were in Germany at the outbreak of the war and it was some time before they reached England. The difficulties they experienced in getting home supplied the basic idea of my revue. Leaving Berlin, they travelled for a day or so, when suddenly they were put out of the train and kept at a station —the name of which they did not know—for a day or so more. They were put on another train, and the same thing happened. How many frontiers they crossed they could never tell. "When we reached England," one of them told me, "I had no idea that I was in England until I heard the English-speaking porters."

'That gave me the idea. I approached several authors, and began to despair of finding one who grasped what I wished to present. Then I thought of Harry Grattan, and dug him out of some rooms in Lower Regent Street. In a few days the revue was complete, and we produced it with no attempt at scenery, just plain black curtains. That alone was a departure for the London stage.

'The opening scene showed the Ambassadors stage quite bare save for a table, at which sat Mr. J. M. Campbell in the role of the stage doorkeeper of a deserted theatre at a seaport town. The revue began by his reading of a letter from the proprietor of the theatre, who was at the front. For ten minutes at least Campbell kept the audience in roars at the humorous topical sallies written by Mr. Grattan. Then one saw, through the actual stage door of the Ambassadors' Theatre, porters bringing in baskets, boxes, and the other paraphernalia of a travelling troupe. The porters were followed by the troupe itself, headed by Max Dearly. All rushed up to the stage doorkeeper, clamouring to him in every language but English. The stage doorkeeper, nonplussed, blurted out in the vernacular of the stage-hand a very obvious English phrase. There was a chorus of "Where are we?" The follow-on was obvious. "Here's a theatre—we are players—let's give a show. What can we do?" And it was Max Dearly who got a laugh by saying, "Why, we have some English dancers, so why not give a French revue?" So started what I consider was the best revue ever presented in London.

'On the opening night the theatre was filled with the usual first-night audience composed of dramatic critics, managers, agents, players, and theatrical hangers-on. The lack of scenery, the entirely new form of entertainment, the obvious economy, left the audience in blank dismay. The critics, the next day, either damned us by leaving us alone or by cutting us to ribbons. One paper said, "Of *Odds and Ends* it would be kinder to say nothing!" I had put in the programme the following words: "Mr. Charles B. Cochran has spared no economy in mounting this revue." A Scotch dramatic critic pointed out that I should employ somebody who would not permit me to use the word "economy' when evidently I meant "expense".

'Often I have accepted defeat at the hands of an audience, and said to myself at the end of the first performance, "They're right. How is it I didn't see it before?" This time I was quite sure that the verdict of the first-night audience and the dramatic critics was at fault. I had conceived an entertainment which was too new, too revolutionary, and I had to find my audience.

'I was, as I thought, alone in the theatre after the audience had left, when Mr. Waddington of Webster & Waddington, the well-known theatre ticket agents, found me out and said, "Cochran, if you persevere with this you will have a success." I have always been grateful to him for these words, which I felt in my own heart were right.

'And so it proved. Business was not wonderful. We started by playing to houses from £25 to £30 a night. Gradually the receipts rose to £40. I found that the people I believed I should attract were coming to my theatre and were coming again and again. On one night, in the first month of the run, I saw in the stalls Lord D'Abernon, Mrs. Asquith, Lady Diana Manners, Augustus John, Philippe de Vilmorin, and a large number of interesting people. I resolved to have another bid for the press, so I put in a new scene, and invited them all over again. This time I rigorously kept out the usual first-night audience other than the critics, and carefully spread the critics among the paying public. In a little theatre like the Ambassadors, to have sitting together five or six people who don't laugh or applaud is demoralising. The house was filled with regular customers who had seen the revue over and over again, and everything went with a rattle and a roar from start to finish.

'The notices the next day were as enthusiastic as, on the first occasion, they were damning. *Odds and Ends* ran for nearly five hundred nights, and I made a profit of £500 a week.'

Cochran omits to say that *Odds and Ends* was only part of the evening's bill. It was originally preceded by two one-act plays in French and English, and then by changes of bill during the run. It was followed by a full evening's revue *More (Odds and Ends)* (1916) and *Pell Mell* (1917).

The new St. Martin's Theatre, next door to the Ambassadors, was now built and ready for occupation and Cochran took a 21 years' lease, opening on 23 November 1916. He tells in his book:

'My opening production was a musical comedy, *Houp-La*, by Fred Thompson and Hugh F. Wright, with music by Nat D. Ayer and Howard Talbot; and the theatre world generally, and the West End in particular, were unusually interested because I began by charging a guinea for the stalls . . . I abandoned the experiment of the guinea stalls after the first week. It was not so much that the policy was wrong for a small theatre with big "stars", as that the show was not up to the guinea mark. Had I instituted guinea stalls during the run of *More* at the Ambassadors I think the experiment would have been successful . . . *Houp-La* created a demand for the high-priced chorus-girl and show-lady. Alfred Butt instructed his lieutenants to get the pick of my girls from the St. Martin's, even if they cost double the salary of the ordinary chorus-girl. . . . In *Houp-La* I introduced a more complete French revue than I had done in *More* at the Ambassadors. The *compère*, Miss Vera Neville, and the *commère*, Miss Valerie May, were dreams of beauty. I fancy that the beautiful legs of Miss Neville sold many a stall. And she had never worn tights before! At the dress rehearsal Gertie Millar had to show her how to put them on, and how to keep the wrinkles out.'

Cochran's own ambiguity as to the name with which to designate the style of the show is typical of a number of productions of this period, which call themselves 'Musical Comedy Revue', 'One of those Musical Things' and other such hybrids.

C.B.C. adds: 'The salaries of Delysia and Morton had now outgrown the capacity of the Ambassadors Theatre. Within a few weeks of her opening with me in *Odds and Ends* Delysia was receiving offers from other managements. She had no written contracts with me . . . The Ambassadors would not stand three-figure salaries, together with the costly productions it was now compelled to put on to keep pace with the numerous small revues that were being presented at other theatres. I decided therefore to abandon revue for a time.'

In 1917 he had produced £500 'A war economy revue' at the St. Martin's! While he was working in other branches of theatre, intimate revue was looked after by André Charlot from the Alhambra, who had seen a future in the new style and began to copy Cochran's methods. On the strength of the success of *Samples*, produced at the Playhouse in November 1915, Charlot took over the Vaudeville Theatre and commenced a long series of revues which brought stardom to so many up and coming new names, Binnie Hale, Beatrice Lillie and Gertrude Lawrence among them. Their names will evoke memories among older theatre-goers, *Some* (1916), *Cheep* (1917), *Tabs* (1918), *Buzz-Buzz* (1918), *Just Fancy* (1920), *Jumble Sale* (1920), *Puss-Puss* (1921), *Pot Luck* (1921), *Snap* (1922), *Rats* (1923), *Yes* (1923). Besides these Charlot had successes at the Comedy Theatre with *This and That*, *See-Saw* both in 1916, *Bubbly* (1917) and *Tails-Up* (1918).

It was in this last revue that the young Noël Coward made his first appearance on a West-end programme as a lyric writer. Phyllis Titmus sang 'Peter Pan', lyric by Noël Coward with music by Doris Joel.

Before the Great War ended Cochran was to re-enter the world of revue when he took over the London Pavilion in 1918. He stripped this world famous music hall of its familiar decorations, making it his headquarters and 'The Centre of the World', as he announced in lights, and famous for revue for the next decade. His opening production, *As You Were* from Rip's *Plus ça Change*, inevitably starred Alice Delysia, dressed by Paul Poiret. Not for the first time was C.B.C. in conflict with the critics and the Censor.

'At the dress rehearsal people associated with the production, the costumiers, the scene painters, and other folk with experience of the stage, were stunned with the beauty of the dresses in the Court of Hunzollern scene. It never occurred to anybody that they were going to create protest. But they did. One critic said, "The ladies of the Court are alike afflicted with *embonpoint*. This may have been meant as satire on German grossness, but the giggles of the audience proved that a different interpretation could be put, and was, on this unsightly and indelicate joke."

'Why these Hunzollern dresses upset the critics I could never understand. I never met a member of the audience who was shocked by them. The Lord Chamberlain, stirred up by the press, requested me to alter the dresses. I was not at all willing to do so, but ultimately I modified them. As Lucifer, Delysia wore a skin-tight black costume. In the light of what has been worn in London since, it is amusing to think of the storm which this costume caused. Delysia looked most attractive in it. I often wonder why it is that dramatic critics have such a dislike for the female form, which the average man finds most attractive.

'Delysia was much amused by the hubbub about her dresses, and frankly she could not understand the attitude of these critics. To one interviewer she said, "I wonder what your English critics really mean when they speak of this frock as "daring". If they mean "improper", "indecent", then I am angry. They say my back is bare—that it is too bare. It seems then that decency is to be estimated in square inches. Really I have no patience; but I have proof, by my reception every night, that it is not my audience that objects to my frocks. I know your Mrs. Grundy; but then she's not a playgoer."

'At this epoch the London stage was rampant with vulgarity which passed unheeded by the censor, and I was truly indignant that my beautiful costumes should be criticised when coarseness of a kind which I would never permit upon my stage was tolerated and applauded at very many London theatres. But the mind of the stage censor in England has always been like that. You may be vulgar, you may be coarse, but when a manager thinks to introduce beauty and wit he is on dangerous ground.'

As the war finished and victory celebrations crowded in so the names of revues reflected the times with *Joy-Bells!* at the Hippodrome and *Back Again* at the Ambassadors, while on tour it was a free for all with *Demobilised* at the Imperial, Canning Town, *The Great 1919 Victory Revue* at Blackpool, *Little Miss Mufti* at Portsmouth, *Sweet Fanny Adams* at Redcliffe, and *Lights Up* at West Bromwich (a title to be used by Cochran in the next war).

The troops in Flanders had often made their own entertainment and *Les Rouges et Noirs*, the First Army Entertainers, under the direction of Captain Eliot Makeham were to make history as the revue *Splinters*. 'This unique organisation was the leading troupe officially recognised by Army headquarters, that cheered the spirits and provided amusement for our war-worn soldiers on the battlefields of France.' In August 1919 the all-male company appeared in *Splinters* at the Savoy Theatre, led by Eliot Makeham with Reg Stone as 'leading lady', but London's West End was not yet ready for a 'drag' show. (The same can still be said as *Birds of a Feather* 'failed to attract' at the Royalty Theatre in 1970.) *Splinters* was to be handed down the generations on tour until 1938—almost the outbreak of yet another war. The prescription was then once more dispensed for the 'ailments' of the troops, and Hal Jones, who had been *Splinters* principal comedian from the original days, moved on into E.N.S.A. and *We Were in the Forces*.

THE YEARS BETWEEN

With the end of the 1914-18 war, and revue established in many West-end theatres, some of the older managements, who had for years looked to musical comedy to provide audiences for the lighter stage, began to take stock of the new situation. George Edwardes had died and his successors were safe at the Gaiety Theatre and at Daly's Theatre with José Collins as their star attraction. The rebuilt Middlesex Music Hall of 1911 was re-decorated and became the Winter Garden Theatre, under Grossmith and Laurillard, in 1919 and the home of a long series of musical comedy successes. Cochran, firmly established at the London Pavilion, in 1921 re-constructed the old Oxford Music Hall as the New Oxford Theatre and presented the Dolly Sisters in a big spectacular revue *League of Notions*. His trump card, Delysia, was there in 1922 in *Mayfair in Montmartre*, but after this Cochran concentrated on the Pavilion and the Oxford gradually sank into oblivion. The old fashioned music halls like the Tivoli had vanished. The London Palladium gradually went over to revue under Charles Gulliver, followed by the Victoria Palace, while the Alhambra alternated. Only the London Coliseum and the Holborn Empire remained faithful to variety.

New sophisticated writers and composers were to emerge to take the place of the original creators of more commonplace revue 'books' and music.

After several small contributions to revues Noël Coward was given his head by Charlot to write *London Calling*, in collaboration with Ronald Jeans, in 1923. Coward provided almost the entire score. He followed this in 1925 with *On With the Dance* and *This Year of Grace* in 1928, both for Cochran, and established his domination of the London revue scene.

André Charlot now entrenched himself at the Prince of Wales' Theatre in a series of revues from 1924, mainly the work of Ronald Jeans but with contributions from many sources including the young Ivor Novello. It was *Charlot's London Revue of 1924* which took New York by storm and introduced Gertrude Lawrence, Beatrice Lillie and Jack Buchanan to Broadway and at last established intimate revue on the other side of the Atlantic. The book was compiled from earlier Charlot successes though mainly by Coward[3]. The Prince of Wales' Theatre for some years became almost a theatre for 'Repertory Revue' as companies and their stars crossed and recrossed the Atlantic and exchanged numbers.

The Co-optimists, originally sub-titled 'A Midsummer Night Scream,' a semi-Pierrot revue, took the place of *The Follies* and became an established part of London 'after dinner' entertainment for almost a decade, and was revived several times well into the thirties. Jack Hulbert and Cicely Courtneidge, forsaking musical comedy, founded a new home for revue at the Little Theatre in the Adelphi, but they moved on to larger theatres and greater fame in 1925 with *By the Way* at the Apollo Theatre, *Clowns in Clover* 1927 and *The House that Jack Built* 1929 at the Adelphi Theatre, but after *Folly to be Wise* at the Piccadilly Theatre in 1931, the 'Talkies' claimed the Hulberts for many years.

The Little Theatre was to remain the home of little revues eventually under

Herbert Farjeon. Nigel Playfair, at the Lyric Theatre, Hammersmith, gave London a more highbrow 'Entertainment in Three Parts' mostly by A. P. Herbert, called *Riverside Nights*, in 1929. Even the repertory movement had provided *Hello Repertory*, from Liverpool, as early as 1915. The London Palladium series brought many more names from the fast vanishing Halls into the fashionable medium. By now all shades of taste had been covered!

The name of the management, or producer as he then preferred to be called, was the hallmark followed by the public, and was to remain so even when the author or composer became of equal importance as the twenties merged into the thirties. But, as with all theatre ventures riding on the crest of a wave, soon all was not as it should be. Cochran with his opulent flair for mixing ballet of high rank with the work of famous painters and artists of worldwide reputation was not without his failures and bankruptcies, though he resiliently rose again. Charlot's liabilities were said to be £60,000 by the Official Receiver in 1931.

The fundamental trouble was blamed on the new medium, the Talkies, which hit London in 1929. The Wireless of the early twenties had had little effect on the theatre, only on variety.

To try and help save live entertainment London went 'Non-Stop' mad with everything from variety and revue to grand guignol, theatre after theatre succumbing to the craze.

An *Evening News* correspondent in November 1932 wrote:

'Queer business altogether, this Non-Stop Entertainment fashion. One house will make hundreds a week out of it, while another a few yards away will lose hundreds.

'As one house decides that it has had enough of Non-Stop and will have no more, another house decides that Non-Stop is *the* thing—and "goes non-stop".

'One week "saucy" scenes and elaborate spectacle are the things that draw the crowd; another week "simplicity" is the magic word.

'A queer business altogether!

'It is just on ten months since the first non-stop "Revudeville" show opened—at the Windmill Theatre, off Piccadilly Circus. That show is still making money, in spite of the just-before-Christmas slump, so I was assured today—and I was shown figures.

'Novelty is the watchword at the Windmill, and something new to continuous revue is now in contemplation for the New Year.

'A hundred yards or so from the Windmill another new non-stop show opens tonight. This is a revue show at the Piccadilly Theatre, the front of which is decorated with pictures of girls and announcements about scenes from the Folies Bergère, with British turns interspersed, and other attractions.

'Close at hand, at the Prince of Wales' Theatre, there is another continuous revue entertainment. Across the way the London Pavilion, which went non-stop in May, sticks to straight variety turns. Down the Strand, the Vaudeville Theatre people have decided to give up non-stop revue in favour of non-stop variety turns. The change takes place on Monday. I was told that the Victoria Palace is "satisfied" with non-stop variety, and will carry on with it even if a season of matinées of *The Windmill Man* is interposed at Christmas.

'At the Phoenix non-stop has ended—in a loss.

'But there are always new enterprises ready to take the place of those which go. Last week the Prince Edward Theatre went non-stop, and next month Mrs. Laura Henderson, who is behind the Windmill Theatre success, has decided to run a non-stop show for a month at the Lyric, Hammersmith.

'Mrs. Henderson did not expect to make a profit out of her Windmill Theatre venture. Her idea was to create employment. But in the last few weeks the "overhead" costs of £525 a week have been exceeded by more than £100 on an average. And that in a little theatre which only holds 300 people.'

Out of it all the Windmill Theatre was to stay. Opened originally with a play in June 1931 it soon turned over to non-stop variety and then *Revudeville* in February 1932, produced by Vivian Van Damm (Mrs. Henderson's, general manager). Their boast 'We never closed' lasted till 1964 when more permissive times made their non-stop nudes a little outmoded.

Similarly the long series of anglicised Folies Bergère revues, mainly at the Prince of Wales' Theatre, as rebuilt in 1937 under Alfred Esdaile, at the London Hippodrome under George Black and the London Casino under Bernard Delfont provide the lineage of the cabaret-restaurants of today.

In the thirties, week in week out, shoddy reproductions and blatant, tasteless imitations were to tour what remained of the suburban and provincial music halls. These, along with 'nude' revues, had a boom period during the second war, financially if not artistically successful. There followed a sad decline of standards with the death throes of the halls in the nineteen-fifties when television took over as the stay-at-home entertainment of the old twice-nightly public.

Cochran had seen the need for change. Writing in 1933 he said:

'Economic conditions [in the theatre] are only now beginning to improve and times like these give us the chance to examine ourselves and ensure that the quality of our work will stand the severest test.

'. . . one must be brief and I intend to confine my examination of modern tendencies to those of the revue, a form of entertainment which always has my interest. I think that revue is an admirable method of expression for the dramatist of today. Not only is the theatre in the melting-pot, but the whole world is also. Conditions of life are changing every time we draw a breath; opinions change even more rapidly. What more natural than that the dramatist should examine, probe and satirise our habits and customs?

'. . . When I first started producing revues in 1913 my aim was to follow the French method closely, making every item as pungent and humorous a commentary as possible on some event. The first author I approached to write a revue was Bernard Shaw. Later, I discussed the idea with H. G. Wells, and, though up to the present I have not persuaded either to go further into the matter, I have not given up hope. As a matter of fact, *The Apple Cart* did not depart much in style from my original conception of English revue.

'One of the best examples of pure *revue* with which I was connected was *As You Were*, done at the London Pavilion in 1918. This was a war-time production, satirising war and profiteers, both in the immediate past and throughout the ages. Unfortunately, the war saw a degeneration in the revue idea. The word lost most of its significance and came to be applied to any entertainment which lacked a plot.

'It was raised on to an entirely different plane with the arrival of Noël Coward. In *This Year of Grace* he maintained a topical note throughout, which, to my mind, was largely responsible for the great success of the show, while the brilliance of his wit and the modernity of his music gave revue-producers the new inspiration they so urgently needed.

'I think the process of unification is the most important element in revue today. It is not enough to pitchfork on to the stage a series of sketches, songs and dances. There must be design and form, balance and rhythm, and the best way to achieve these objects is to put all your eggs in one basket, or, in other words, bank on one man's inspiration and ability to carry out his ideas.

'I believe the revue written and composed by twenty different people, however clever, cannot achieve its principal aim—to comment. When we read a good novel or watch a good play or study a fine newspaper article we want to hear the views of a single person who has something worth while to impart. The Tower of Babel principle in constructing revue can only result in an entertainment which is revue only in name.'

In the late thirties a new revitalising force was to come to intimate revue via the Gate Theatre in Villiers Street, a serious club theatre under Norman Marshall, where 'members' frolics' were to become an institution from which in March 1939 the work of Diana Morgan, Robert Macdermot and the artistry of Hermione Gingold burst on to the West-end public stage to set a pattern for the ensuing years of blackout and beyond, with the name of the director becoming of increasing importance.

THE WAR AND AFTER

As usual light entertainment did well during the war, but this time the serious stage was not so far behind. The surprising thing was the great popularity with the troops of the more sophisticated intimate revues, the formula for which was now emerging. The overall picture for 1939-45, and for a while afterwards, was of the large glossy variety revues, later alternating with variety on its own, regularly at the Palladium, and, after hostilities ceased, at the London Casino and the Adelphi Theatre, sometimes at the London Coliseum, the Palace or the Stoll Theatres. Even the Holborn Empire, until it was blitzed, fell into line.

At the Comedy Theatre Hermione Baddeley, from the Little Revues, and Hermione Gingold, from the Gate Theatre, joined in a partnership which began an amusingly insulting association and was to gather momentum as they individually starred in vehicle after vehicle over the next eight years.

The names of directors, following the lead of Norman Marshall, became of great importance. Charles Hickman, Henry Kendal (also as a performer), Laurier Lister and William Chappell span the next two decades.

Though in 1945 Coward returned to revue with *Sigh No More*, it is the work of Alan Melville, followed in the fifties by Peter Myers, in association with the music of Ronnie Cass, that epitomizes the era.

Throughout the war the *Sweet and Low* series, with its predecessors and followers made the name of the Ambassadors Theatre synonymous with intimate revue. Later the Lyric Theatre, Hammersmith, was to cradle another series of H.M. Tennent productions which infiltrated the West-end over the post-war years. New stars were made overnight and reputations built. It now took many writers and composers to contribute to successful revue; so complex was the authorship that individual praise or blame often became difficult to assess. The popularity achieved by intimate revue after the war was such that it spread to the little clubs and attic theatres in and around London. The Myers-Cass partnership saw the light of day via the New Lindsay Theatre at Notting Hill Gate and at the Irving Theatre in the West-end. New experimental and more integrated productions like *Cranks* came to the West-end from the Watergate Theatre Club and *Share my Lettuce* from the Lyric Theatre, Hammersmith. John Cranko in 1955 and Bamber Gascoigne in 1957 pointed the way to a new path. By now most 'legitimate' West-end managements were 'in on the act'. Linnett and Dunfee, Peter Bridge, Michael Codron and Donald Albery all had revues to their credit.

The public for this smart, sophisticated, inbred parochial humour, which became more and more theatrical and parish pump in its context, seemed unlimited. A revue title, *Hi! Camp*, though strangely never used, would have summed them all up. To a younger generation it all seemed remote and out of touch and devoid of contemporary political or social significance.

Gradually the critics became less and less amused, except when new writers, often bred in television, began to emerge, like John Mortimer, Harold Pinter and N. F. Simpson, but the routine formula was far too predictable. Intimate revue had become like a snake swallowing its own tail.

The London season of the Cambridge University Footlights Revue, *Out of the Blue*, in 1954, produced by Leslie Bricusse, brought Jonathan Miller to the notice of the critics and the general public, and the tares were sown in the revue field for the supplanting of the professional writer by the new amateur satirist with a completely fresh outlook on life and society.

BEYOND AND AFTER THE FRINGE

The new movement found its feet with an Edinburgh Festival late-night fringe revue, conceived and produced by John Bassett in 1960.

Beyond the Fringe brought together Alan Bennett from Oxford University, where he was still teaching as late as 1962; Peter Cook from Cambridge whose work as a writer for The Footlights had taken him into the West-end revue world with *Pieces of Eight* (1959) and later *One Over the Eight* (1961); Jonathan Miller, also from Cambridge, who qualified as a doctor in 1959 and had worked with The Footlights in both London seasons; and lastly Dudley Moore, who left Oxford as a Bachelor of Music in 1958 and joined the 'intellectual jazz scene' via the B.B.C. and incidental music to T.V. documentaries and stage productions.

The quartet thus brought together gave birth to a new form of satirical revue which was eventually to transfer to London under the direction of Eleanor Fazan at the Fortune Theatre. Four young men in ordinary dress, without make-up, on a bare stage save for rostrums, made history overnight.

In his introduction to the published script Michael Frayne says:

'*Beyond the Fringe* first fell upon London like a sweet, refreshing rain on the tenth of May, 1961. It must have been St. Jonathan's Day, because it has rained satire ever since, day and night, harder and harder, spreading outwards from London to cover the whole of the British Isles in one steady downpour of soaking jokes, until, as Peter Cook said recently, the entire realm seems about to sink sniggering beneath the watery main.

'No sociologist, so far as I know, has yet got around to analysing this extraordinary phenomenon. The demand must have existed, ravenous but unrecognised, before the supply was connected, for the public did not have to be coaxed to appreciate *Beyond the Fringe*. They fell upon it deliriously like starving men, sweeping with them in the stampede all sorts of people who can scarcely have had much idea what it was they were devouring.

'God knows', he goes on, 'how the Lord Chamberlain ever came to allow the show to be put on, seeing that it flouts venerable official prejudices of his which he had until then defended to the last drop of asininity. I have heard it suggested that there was a new spirit of enlightenment abroad in the Lord Chamberlain's office. But one wonders, one wonders.

'I don't think that the impact of the show', he adds, 'was entirely due to the fact that it was satirical. Its principal and irresistible recommendation was that it was *funny*—very funny—much funnier than anything the satire business has done since. By no means everything in the show is "satirical", in the sense in which that poor, broken-winded word has come to be understood. Several of the items —Jonathan Miller's monologue on the trousers, for instance—are clearly in the old whimsical-fantastical school of Paul Jennings and *Cranks* in which all humorists of my generation were brought up . . .

'I'm sure it was also largely the sheer surprise of going to a revue and finding oneself addressed not by hired spokesmen, zombies with neatly squared-off, bulled-up theatrical faces, repeating someone else's jokes, but directly, by recognisable human beings, who talked about things that human beings talk about outside the theatre, and not special defunct demonstration topics brought out of the formaldehyde only for revues. It was also, after all the years of being nervously nursed back to sobriety after each joke with torch-songs and *pas de trois* representing jealousy, the grateful shock of finding that the management trusted one not to dislocate one's jaw or be sick over the furnishings if one was allowed to laugh continuously for the whole evening . . .

'Revue had more or less strangled itself in its own clichés; the "Fringe" people were the first in this country with the genuine originality to hack their way right back to first principles and start all over again.'

Frayne also says 'Alan Bennett once told me that they had conceived *Beyond the Fringe* simply by all standing round and deciding what they loathed, then sending it up. It sounds almost too admirably rational to be true.'

The revue, an instantaneous success, ran at the Fortune Theatre until April 1964 totalling 1,184 performances and then transferred to the May Fair Theatre for a further 1,016 performances, with changes of cast and revised or new material at both theatres. The original London company made a similar impact on New York in October 1962.

The effect of the production was soon felt in other quarters. Though the established stars of revue were still at the top of their form and popularity, one after another of the succeeding productions by the 'old hands' who valiantly tried to give a new look to the old formula, either failed or had only a moderate success. Only *Wait a Minim!*, from South Africa, in quite a different style, exploiting native music and instruments, achieved a run of 656 performances at the Fortune Theatre after *Beyond the Fringe* transferred.

By the time *Beyond the Fringe* ended its record run of 2,200 performances in the autumn of 1966 it reigned alone in the West-end.

[37]

From 1966 to 1970 the West-end of London was more or less revueless. The annual variety revues, always a law unto themselves, flourished at the Palladium, and several entertainments which came under the heading of 'An Evening with . . .' came and quickly went.

Peter Myers and Ronnie Cass, always undaunted, carried on the fight for intimate revue both on tour and at the May Fair Theatre. Their second attempt there, *Ten Years Hard*, was nearer the original intention and spirit of *revue* as originally conceived because it endeavoured to satirise the foibles and follies of the past decade. Its theme—Is satire dead?—was over-debated. The company, in funereal black, began by attacking its obsequies, but Satire, personified, sprang from its coffin, alive and kicking. No satisfactory conclusion was reached! It is interesting that this rearguard action opened on 6 July 1970, just twenty-one days before the frontal attack of *Oh! Calcutta!* at the Round House.

The wave of permissiveness was ready to engulf the sexy sixties and the long battle fought by some sections of the entertainment world, to end the domination of the Lord Chamberlain and the power of the censor, was in sight of fulfilment. The end came, and was celebrated with the production of *Hair* at the Shaftesbury Theatre, on 27 September 1968.

The original *Fringe* quartet did not follow up their success, in the theatre, but the gauntlet was taken up by television, outside the Lord Chamberlain's fatherly care, which now became the most popular medium for revue in all its permutations. Most of the established or new comedians appeared in revue-like programmes. Satire found its haven in the work of Ned Sherrin with *That was the Week that was* and *Not so much a Programme, More a Way of Life*. Eventually, as John Barber remarked in his notice of *Ten Years Hard*, 'To-day the very word satire evokes a yawn.' Its juvenile undergraduate parents had almost flogged it to death and it now had to grow up or expire.

The old favourites of intimate revue had a grand return with the two Alan Melville television series *Before the Fringe* which helped, both through its material and its artists, to satisfy a large proportion of the nostalgic older viewers, and introduced a new generation to the wonders of 'the good old days.'

The return of revue at two extremes to the West-end was led, in April 1970, by *At the Palace*, a mixture of cabaret, variety and revue in the age old formula, with a star of magnitude, Danny La Rue, after his long apprenticeship in cabaret and pantomime and the support of Roy Hudd fresh from his television success. Together they brought back to the general public something that had long been absent, wholesome vulgarity!

At the other end of the scale Ken Tynan had conceived a *voyeurs'* picnic, *O, quel cue tu as*, with contributions from many hands, called *Oh! Calcutta!* which had first been seen in New York on 17 June 1969, appropriately at the Eden Theatre. After tentative probes into the permissive climate it eventually made its much heralded entry into London, at the Round House, on 27 July 1970, and transferred to the West-end at the Royalty Theatre on 30 September. Mixing frontery with effrontery it soon found its own public.

With the revue field now left to *At the Palace* and *Oh! Calcutta!* at last the theatre-going public know where they stand! Equal success being achieved by the over-dressed or the over-exposed!

It is not the theatre historian's function to criticise, but to try his best to put into perspective the previous night's 'First night', and hope to do the same thing for tomorrow evening and the night after.

Since *Oh! Calcutta!* there have been attempts to revive intimate revue at little theatres, clubs and pubs, either as a lunch time *hors d'oeuvre* or a late night snack, but it has not again so far been served up as a full course meal.

In New York *Oh! Calcutta!* was followed—off off-Broadway—by *The Dirtiest Show in Town* which reached London in May 1971. Though expressly described by its creator, Tom Eyen, as 'A Documentary' it was received almost unanimously by the critics as 'A Revue'—which may prove to be a signpost erected to the naked road ahead.

---

[1] In New York, between 1893 and 1899, a series of successful summer 'Reviews' were staged at the Casino Theatre but apart from a few inferior copies the form of entertainment did not catch on in America either. [see page 17.]

[2] The Shuberts opened their Winter Garden in 1911 with *La Belle Paris*, and the subsequent success of *The Passing Show of 1912* at last established revue in New York. [see page 26.]

[3] *The Greenwich Village Follies* of 1919, which reached Broadway in 1921, under the direction of John Murray Anderson and later Hassard Short, had paved the way for the British invasion. [see page 32.]

Acknowledgements

The history of revue has so far been neglected by theatrical historians, and even the gossipy writers of the thirties and forties lumped it unceremoniously with either Musical Comedy or Music Hall. Authors like Ernest Short, who wrote *Fifty Years of Vaudeville* (Eyre and Spottiswood 1940), lived through the main era of revue and not only romanticised their memories but created a bottomless mine of inaccuracies, mis-quotations and eccentricities. The history of revue on the other side of the Atlantic is strangely buried but well documented in *Musical Comedy in America* by Cecil Smith (Theatre Arts Books, 1950).

There have also been, and sad to say still are, those journalist-historians who will, at the drop of a coin—if asked—write on any theatrical subject. All previous books and research are their oyster.

The loyal historian must look up and check facts at source; to rely on memory or hearsay is fatal, even to the best intentioned writers. As with *Musical Comedy* we have tried to put the story of revue into perspective, trace its false starts, and give, in pictures, some idea of its content. Revue is harder to define pictorially than the musical. Every playgoer will have his especial memory either of sketch or song. The choice must, perforce, be personal, but we have tried to show examples of all the ingredients which have gone to make up revue.

In our research, as always, we have been helped by the staff of the Enthoven Collection at the Victoria and Albert Museum, particularly Tony Latham, who, as a private chore, read the book in its manuscript and proof stages and gave invaluable advice for which we are deeply indebted.

We also wish to thank Miss Dorothy Dickson for permission to quote from the writings of C. B. Cochran, of which she is the trustee; Souvenir Press for allowing us to quote from Michael Frayne's Introduction to *Beyond the Fringe*.

Press representatives of leading managements, and personal managers, have been unfailing in their courtesy, including Vivienne Byerley, Roger Clifford and Jack Hanson. The following photographers' work is reproduced: Houston Rogers, Nos. 202, 203, 204, 205, 206, 207, 208, 211, 217, 219 and 220. Angus McBean (Harvard University Collection) Nos. 169, 173, 192, 193, 194, 197, 198, 199, 212, 215 and 216. Tom Hustler, Nos. 222 and 223. Trans World Eye, Nos. 224 and 225. Lewis Morley, No. 218. Also the following pictures from the Enthoven Collection, Nos. 6 and 8.

As ever we have to thank Frances Fleetwood for the index, Mary Quinnell for her patience (tried, she says, more than we will ever realise!!!) with our hieroglyphics, which pass for a manuscript. Vera Seaton Reid for her inevitable material assistance, Edward J. Wood for his usual advice, Gil de Lesparda for tracing the origin of the Montaigne quotation and Robert Baker for looking over our proofs with a professional school-mastery eye.

Last, and most especially, our loving thanks to Sir Noël Coward for his Foreword.

1. *Above.* Charles Mathews and Frederick Yates Entertainment. Adelphi Theatre, April 1831. The two comedians in some of the varied characters they assumed during the course of the evening in their *At Home.*

2. *Left.* Frances Maria Kelly as Mrs Parthian in Part Three of her Entertainment *Dramatic Recollections with Studies of Character.* Royal Strand Subscription Theatre, 1833.

Mrs Parthian at Home
The Music selected from the Compositions of
Mr T. Cooke.

Characters

Sally Simkin, (with snatches of Ballads
   and a very original Kit-Cat Song) .. Miss KELLY!
Mrs Parthian, (as well as her memory
   serves her) .... Miss KELLY!
Miss Betsy Rattle, (a desirable Inmate
   for unfurnished apartments) ...... Miss KELLY!
Mademoiselle Jejeune, (a Governess and
   Actress elect) .... Miss KELLY!
The Blind Boy .... Miss KELLY!
The Dumb Girl.................... Miss KELLY!
Miss Kelly, by .... Miss KELLY!

3. *Above. The Drama at Home! or, an Evening with Puff* by J. R. Planché. Theatre Royal, Haymarket, 1844. Julia Glover as the muse of Drama in her ruined shrine is revived by Charles James Mathews as Mr Puff.

4. *Below. Mr Buckstone's Voyage Round the Globe (i Leicester Square)* by J. R. Planché. Theatre Royal Haymarket, 1854.

'The opportunity for the introduction of "a Gran Oriental Spectacle" is naturally seized; and the Danc of the Bayadères exhibits to great advantage th attractions of the *corps de ballet* and the skill of Mis Lydia Thompson and Miss L. Morris. It is in creatin such opportunities, and in skilfully improving them that the merit of this peculiar sort of drama consists.

Above. The New Haymarket Spring Meeting 1855 by J. R. Planché. Theatre Royal, Haymarket, 1855. The opening scene. J. B. Buckstone as the Lord Mayor's Fool introduces the City of Westminster, Caroline White, to the City of London, Harriett Gordon, in Guildhall.

'The matter of complaint against the City is, that within its walls it fails to encourage the stage, and that people must go as far as Norton Folgate for a theatre. This civic prejudice is old enough to be obsolete; and the rejection of the drama, so that it has to find refuge in extramural establishments, is anything but creditable to the intelligence of the authorities. The City of London ought, as a duty, to have a model theatre for the high drama, and might do much good in this way, and find beneficial occupation for funds now wasted.'

Below. 1863; or, the Sensations of the Past Season with Shameful Revelation of 'Lady Somebody's Secret' by Henry James Byron. St James's Theatre, 1863.

Paul Bedford as George Tallboys is pushed down the well by J. L. Toole as Lady Audley in a burlesque of *Lady Audley's Secret*, The 'Sensation' of the past season.

7. *Above left. Under the Clock* by Seymour Hicks and Charles Brookfield. Royal Court Theatre, 1893. Charles Brookfield as Sherlock Holmes.

8. *Right.* Seymour Hicks in *Under the Clock.* Royal Court Theatre, 1893.

9. *Left. Pot-Pourri,* 'A "Revue" of 1899' by James L. Tanner. Avenue Theatre, 1899. Marie Dainton in a burlesque of Irene Vanbrugh as Sophy Fullgarney manicuring in *The Gay Lord Quex.*

10. *Left. Rogues and Vagabonds* by George Grossmith. Empire Theatre, 1905. Sybil Arundale as Harlequin who acted as compère throughout in various guises. The rest of the cast included Marie Dainton, Harry Grattan, W. H. Berry, Fred Farren and Arthur Playfair, with scenes in 'A Subway Station' and 'Aldwych'; it was produced by Tom Terriss.

. *Right. The 'Revue'* by Victor de Cottens. London oliseum, 1906, which had both a compère and a mmère. Billie Burke as the commère sang

Elegance, chic and dainty grace
Added to style refined—yet free,
    Radiance splendid
    Happily blended
With an alluring modesty,
Such are the charms for which I'm noted,
To me the men are all devoted.'

12. *Above. Venus—1906* by George Grossmith. Empire Theatre, 1906. Daisy Cordell as Venus, Sybil Arundale as Lord Percy Pall Mall, Elizabeth Firth as the Gibson Girl and T. Tremayne as Vulcan.

'The idea underlying the revue seems to be the triumph of the older Venus over the newer type exhibited in the monstrously-shapen Gibson Girl of our time and the rise of Labour in the shape of Vulcan, who in the fourth scene smashes Trafalgar Square to atoms.'

The revue had two numbers by Jerome Kern.

13. *Below. Hullo . . . London!* by George Grossmith. Empire Theatre, 1910. The Caterer, J. F. McArdle, is fascinated by a giver of classical dances for charity, Maud Jay in a burlesque of Lady Constance Stewart-Richardson, who, when she says she only dances for charity is asked, 'Then why not dance where charity begins?'

Two long remembered songs, 'Shine on harvest moon' and 'I've got rings on my fingers', were first heard in this revue.

14. *Right.* George Grossmith, 1908. At this time 'Junior', his father, the famous 'Entertainer at the Piano' and creator of most of the comedy parts in the Gilbert and Sullivan operas, was still alive. Even the father had been 'Junior' in his day, as the first George Grossmith had been in the public eye as a lecturer.

The third Grossmith made his name in musical comedy under George Edwardes both as actor and writer. He was the author of the first Empire revue and of several of those that followed. He first appeared in Paris in *revue* as the typical English 'dude' in 1910 at the Folies Bergère and later at other theatres there.

15. *Below. By George!* by George Grossmith. Empire Theatre, 1911. The 'Coronation Revue' of George V 'has burlesqued nearly everyone and everything that has attracted attention during the past year. *By George!* also projects itself into the future, and we get further fun from that.'

16. *The Follies* Company, Apollo Theatre, 1908. Norman Blumé, Dan Everard, H. G. Pélissier, Muriel George, Gwennie Mars, Lewis Sydney and Ethel Allandale. Harry Pélissier both wrote and directed *The Follies*.

17. *Above. The Follies*, Apollo Theatre, 1911, in one of Pélissier's 'Potted Plays', *Henry VIII*, a burlesque of Beerbohm Tree's Coronation revival at His Majesty's Theatre. Douglas Maclaren (Earl of Surrey), Morris Harvey (Henry VIII), Dan Everard (Buckingham), Ethel Allandale (Anne Bullen), Lewis Sydney (Lord Chamberlain), Gwennie Mars (Queen Katherine), R. Brighten Salisbury (Cromwell), H. G. Pélissier (Wolsey).

18. *Below. All Change Here*, Alhambra Theatre, 1911. A Pélissier revue of the year 1910 in a variety bill. It included a burlesque of Richard Strauss's *Elektra* at Covent Garden when the audience implored the composer to give them melody.

19. *Left. C'Est Chic*, Middlesex Theatre of Varieties, 1913. 'The Dance of the Black Pearl', a poster which was banned by the Censorship Committee of the Bill-Posters' Association. At the time it was said:
'The original is printed in black and white and pink; and it is possibly the last of these three colours which the bill-posters, sticking fast to their principles, do not consider the pink of perfection.'

20. *Right.* Mlle Serrana as the Black Pearl: 'Pearls are very much to the fore just now: we have the mystery of the Pearl Necklace, *The Pearl Girl* at the Shaftesbury, and a Pearl Ballet, *C'Est Chic*, at the Middlesex Music Hall. Mlle Serrana dances both behind and before the footlights; in the latter case, on a flower-edged platform passing the front of the stalls.'

21. *Above. J'Adore..Ca!..*, Middlesex Theatre of Varieties, 1913. *Les Eglantines.* A troupe from the Théâtre Ba-Ta-Clan in '*La Rose de Hollande*'.

22. *Below. Cachez Ca! . . .*, Middlesex Theatre of Varieties, 1913. A living poster inspired by the banning of the earlier bill. In the scene 'A bashful bill poster, scared by the immodesty of modern posters, has invented a label which he affixes on all posters that are, according to his ideas, too risky. Several incidents follow.'

23. *Hullo, Rag-time!*, London Hippodrome, 1912. Shirley Kellogg leads the chorus down the joy plank in 'Rag-Time Soldier Man' in an Albert de Courville revue written in collaboration with Max Pemberton, with music by Louis Hirsch. Directed by Austen Hurgon.

24. *Above. Hullo, Rag-time!*. Lew Hearn and
Bonita sing 'Hitchy Koo' in the final scene in
'The Exhibition Grounds'.

25. *Right.* Ethel Levey in *Hullo, Rag-time!*
gives an impersonation of Pavlova in 'The
Bacchanale Rag'.

26. *Left*. Teddie Gerard, from New York, who made her name in London when she succeeded Shirley Kellogg in *Hullo, Rag-time!*. She remained in West-end revues up to the 'twenties.

27. *Right*. *Hullo, Tango!*, London Hippodrome, 1913. A de Courville revue by the same team as before. Ethel Levey wearing a Léon Bakst designed dress as Countess Zicka in 'Hiplomacy', a parody of Sardou's *Diplomacy*.

28. *Above.* Shirley Kellogg and the chorus, dressed by Léon Bakst, sing 'Who's the lady?' in *Hullo, Tango!*.

Right. Harry Tate in *Hullo, Tango!* gives an ˙rsonation of how George Robey would play ˙s own sketch 'Golfing'.

30. *Above. Kill that Fly!* by George Grossmith. Alhambra Theatre, 1912. Muriel Hudson sings a ragtime medley in 'The Metropolitan Cabaret' scene. A skit on the contemporary 'Cave of the Calf', a cabaret theatre club and early London 'night spot'. Directed by Grossmith, André Charlot and M. V. Leveaux.

31. *Left. 8d A Mile* 'The New Stop Press Revue' by George Grossmith and Fred Thompson. Alhambra Theatre, 1913. Ella Retford singing 'All the girls are lovely by the seaside', by Willy Redstone.

32. 'The Spider's Web' by Theodor Kosloff, a dance in *8d A Mile*. Carlotta Mossetti as the Spider and Phyllis Monkman as the Butterfly 'are very agile in climbing about the web and accomplish feats that are quite acrobatic'.

33. *Above. Not Likely!* by George Grossmith and Cosmo Gordon Lennox. Alhambra Theatre, 1914. 'The Sloping Path' and Teddie Gerard sings 'Pass along' by Harry Tierney.

34. *Left.* George Grossmith and Eileen Molyneux in the 'Danse Jarva' in *Not Likely!*. The revue title reflects the impact of Shaw's *Pygmalion* on other entertainments.

35. *Right.* Lee White, who came to London from New York in 1913 and was with the Alhambra revues, *Keep Smiling, Not Likely!, 5064 Gerrard* and *Now's the Time* and followed André Charlot to the Vaudeville Theatre in his later intimate revues.

Francis, Day & Hunter.
REG? N? 257, 748.
Sixpence Nett.

N? 1077 SIXPENNY POPULAR EDITION. (NO DISCOUNT ALLOWED.)

LAST NIGHT WAS THE END OF THE WORLD.

SUNG BY
SAFFO ARNAW

WRITTEN BY
Andrew B. Sterling.

Composed by
HARRY VON TILZER.

IN CARR'S WILD WEST SONG REVUE.

"WHILE YOU WAIT."

SUCCESSFUL SONGS
FEATURED IN THIS REVUE

"YOU MADE ME LOVE YOU". ....
"TRAIL OF THE LONESOME PINE". ....
"CROSS THE MASON DIXON LINE". ....
"SAILING DOWN THE CHESAPEAKE BAY."
"GOOD-BYE BOYS". ....
"LAST NIGHT WAS THE END OF THE WORLD".
"TAKE ME TO THAT SWANEE SHORE". ....
"SUNSHINE AND ROSES". ....
"I LOVE HER (OH! OH! OH!)". ....
"FLOATING DOWN THE RIVER". ....
"BRING ME BACK MY LOVIN' HONEY BOY". ..

London: FRANCIS, DAY & HUNTER,
(For all Countries except America, Canada and Australasia)
142, CHARING CROSS ROAD AND 22, DENMARK STREET, W.C.
New York: THE HARRY VON TILZER MUSIC PUBLISHING C? 125, WEST 43RD STREET.

Copyright MCMXII. { In all Countries (except America, Canada and Australasia) by Francis, Day & Hunter.
In United States of America by The Harry Von Tilzer Music Publishing C?

36. *Above.* While You Wait, a touring 'Wild West' revue, 1912, which hit the London dates at Wood Green Empire in October 1913. The lyric of the song sung by Saffo Arnaw had little of the Wild West about it:

'And then the stars grew dim and cold,   My dream is o'er, to live no more,
The moon grew pale, my heart grew old,   Last night was the end of the world.'

37. *Above.* *The Honeymoon Express*, a touring revue which played the music halls and reached the Oxford in 1914. It was staged by Ned Wayburn.

38. *Below.* Poster for *Venus Ltd.* A touring revue which opened at the Empire, Liverpool in 1914 and reached Finsbury Park Empire the following year.

39. *Above. A Mixed Grill* by W. H. Risque. Empire Theatre, 1914. 'A Bur-revue-lesque' with music by Howard Talbot and directed by Fred Farren. 'A musical-comedy joy-dream' supper at Romano's.

40. *Below left.* Ida Crispi as Lloyd George *A Mixed Grill.* An imagined rehearsal Granville Barker revue in the cooling-room a Turkish bath!

41. *Below.* Phyllis Monkman in *5064 Gerr* Alhambra Theatre, 1915. 'The Zig-Zag Dan

42. *Right.* Gaby Deslys in *5064 Gerrard*, a revue which had several authors and composers and ran into two editions. Gaby Deslys and her partner, Harry Pilcer, danced in the scene 'At Murray's Club' in the second edition. She had just concluded an unsuccessful engagement at the Duke of York's Theatre in a burlesque by James Barrie—*Rosy Rapture, the Pride of the Beauty Chorus* with music by Herman Darewski and Jerome Kern. Some of Darewski's numbers were used in the revue.

43. *Left.* Robert Hale in *5064 Gerrard* as Gaby Deslys in the same scene, 'The Two Gabys', in which the short run of Barrie's show was burlesqued. The author was asked:

'You like my dress?'
'Witty'.
'How do you mean—witty?'
'Do ye ken that brevity is the soul of wit?'

44. *Right.* Elsie Janis in *The Passing Show* by Arthur Wimperis. Palace Theatre, 1914. An Alfred Butt revue. In the opening scene, 'The World's Bazaar', she appeared as Kitty O'Hara 'a colleen who wants to see life'. In the same scene Clara Beck, as a military maid, sang Herman Finck's 'I'll make a man of any one of you', which was to become, when war broke out four months after the opening, one of the most famous of recruiting songs.

45. *Left.* Basil Hallam as Gilbert the Filbert in the opening scene of *The Passing Show*. The song, by Herman Finck, was to. become famous:

'Gilbert, the Filbert, the Knut with a "K",
The pride of Piccadilly, the blasé roué.
Oh, Hades! the ladies who leave their
                                    wooden huts
For Gilbert, the Filbert, the Col'nel of the
                                    Knuts.'

In the same character he was to sing 'The Constant Lover' in the second edition, *The Passing Show of 1915*, before he was killed on active service.

46. *Above. The Passing Show, 'Salle des Tapisseries Anciennes'.* The ballet scene in which 'Five of the figures in the tapestry picture behind the dancers are represented by living ladies'. A variation, in revue, of the *Tableau vivant* which had long been an attraction at the Palace Theatre in its variety days.

47. *Below. By Jingo, If We Do—!* by Arthur Wimperis and Hartley Carrick, with music by Herman Finck. Empire Theatre, 1914. An Alfred Butt revue produced soon after the outbreak of war which reflected the times in both title and content.
James Godden, Fred Groves and Ralph Lynn in an Embankment coffee-stall sketch.

48. *Above.* *Watch Your Step* by H. B. Smith with music and lyrics by Irving Berlin. Empire Theatre, 1915. An anglicised version, by Harry Grattan, of a New York revue.
The 'Metropolitan Opera House' scene, with Joseph Coyne, Ethel Levey and George Graves, during the course of which Phyllis Bedells and the *corps de ballet* danced an excerpt from *Les Sylphides* in true Empire tradition.

49. *Below.* *Joy-Land!* by Albert de Courville and Wal Pink. London Hippodrome, 1915. The opening scene, the 'Landing Stage, Liverpool'. The Last Aboard—Harry Tate.
'The "Big Liner", a huge piece of stage property that was built in three weeks under a railway arch at Peckham; no ordinary workshop was big enough.'

50. *Above. Joy-Land!*, Shirley Kellogg as the Tulip Girl, with the chorus, sings 'In Tulip Time' by Herman Darewski.
'The gangway [Joy] plank across the centre of the house used in *Joy-Land!* is a much more solid affair than the gangways in previous Hippodrome revues. The present structure is made of iron girders, spans and rails—a solid piece of engineering in fact, strong enough to support a light engine.'

51. *Below. Flying Colours!* by Albert de Courville and Wal Pink. London Hippodrome, 1916.
'The Dancing Carnival', sixth tableau. Apache, Tango and Bunny Hug, at the end of which Little Tich danced a Serpentine Dance and Dorothy Ward followed with a ragtime song.

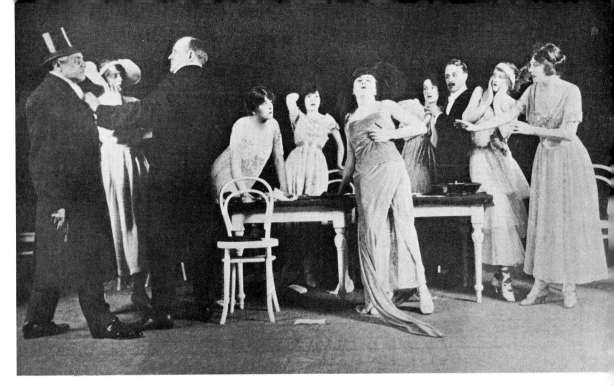

52. *Left.* Alice Delysia first appeared in London in 1914 for Charles B. Cochran, at the Ambassadors Theatre in his first intimate revue *Odds and Ends*, 'A miniature revue' as part of a triple bill.

Its success led to a second and third edition as a full evening's entertainment, *More (Odds and Ends)* in 1915 and 1916. The material was mostly by Harry Grattan, who also directed, with music by Edward Jones.

In the final edition Delysia sang '*Le Rêve passe*' a dramatic song by Charles Helman and George Krier, to the words of A. Foucher.

53. *Above. More (Odds and Ends)*, 1915. 'The Gambling Hell'—'Dramatic Scene' with Morris Harvey (the villain), J. M. Campbell (the husband) and Alice Delysia (the victim).

54. *Right.* Leon Morton in *More (Odds and Ends)* as the Handsome Man in a mime 'Mid-Victorian episode'.

55. *Above. Shell Out!* by Albert de Courville and Wal Pink, with music by Herman Darewski. Comedy Theatre, 1915. Fred Emney as the Waiter and Tom Shale as a Customer who asks 'I wonder if I could manage a little Camembert' and gets the reply 'Not single-handed, you couldn't'.

56. *Below. Shell Out!* The final line-up—Mona Desmond, Larry Ceballos, Edna Morgan, Tom Stuart, Unity More, Fred Emney, Amy Augarde, Garry Lynch, Hilda Bayley, Tom Shale, Louie Tinsley and George Manton.

57. *Above. Vanity Fair* by Arthur Wimperis. Palace Theatre, 1916. An Alfred Butt revue directed by J. A. E. Malone.
Arthur Playfair as Two-Chinned-Chow and Nelson Keys as Zehrat Al Kulub in a burlesque of Oscar Asche and Lily Brayton in *Chu-Chin-Chow.*

58. *Right. Vanity Fair.* Regine Flory and Nelson Keys sing Jerome Kern's 'Some sort of somebody', with words by Elsie Janis, in a white garden.

59. *Above. Zig-Zag!*, a de Courville revue. London Hippodrome, 1917. George Robey 'gives a delightful burlesque of the methods of Fregoli, and other quick-change artists. He emerges from behind the scenes, by turns, as a jealous husband reading his wife's letter to a lover, as the lover, as the butler, and as Signor Peperinello, "de great-a detec-a-tif from Scotlande". The photograph is, of course, a composite one. At one end of the screen Mr Robey appears as the quick-change professor "as in himself he really is"; at the other end as the fickle wife who "wants to be good"—a skit on Miss Doris Keane as Cavallini in *Romance*.'

60. *Left.* Shirley Kellogg in *Zig-Zag!*. The 'Chinese Lacquer' scene, as Shir Lee singing 'Beware of Chu-Chin-Chow' by Dave Stamper.

61. *Above*. Beatrice Lillie in *Cheep* by Harry Grattan. A Charlot revue. Vaudeville Theatre, 1917. 'She is very amusing in the "Dedleighdul" Quartette scene (a travesty of an amateur concert), as a musician of the long-haired kind, and also as a lady performer. In the Bairnsfather scene she makes a charming Canadian soldier who, in his dug-out, dreams of mother and home and sings, "When I am with her again". On the first night the song drew from a sympathetic member of the audience the exclamation, "I'll go with you, kid!" She is also shown in Scene IV, "A Medley", whereof the programme says: "Beatrice Lillie sings about Julia".'

62. *Right*. Gertie Millar as a Jumping Jack sings 'Toy Town' by Lionel Monckton in *Bric-à-Brac*. Palace Theatre, 1915. An Alfred Butt revue by Arthur Wimperis and Basil Hood.

63. *Left*. Roy Royston and Gina Palerme as a Little Nut and a French girl 'On the tiles', join in the duet 'One kiss leads to another' by Herman Finck, in *Bric-à-Brac*.

64. *Right.* Elsie Janis sings 'I love them all just a little bit' by Dan Kildare in *Hullo America!*, Palace Theatre, 1918. An Alfred Butt revue by John Hastings Turner and various composers. Originally Elsie Janis was partnered by Owen Nares, the matinée idol, who was later succeeded by Maurice Chevalier.

65. *Left.* Elsie Janis sings 'The Jazz Band' by Elsie Janis and Dan Kildare in *Hullo America!*. She was joined by the Palace Girls in 'Jazz' dresses. Her skirts parted to display the Stars and Stripes at the end of the number.

3. *Above. Buzz-Buzz* by Arthur Wimperis
and Ronald Jeans. Vaudeville Theatre, 1918.
Gertrude Lawrence and chorus sing 'I lost my
heart in Maori-land' by Alf Lawrence and
Herman Darewski.

4. *Right.* Nelson Keys burlesques Elsie Janis
and sings 'Red, white and blue' in Charlot's
revue *Buzz-Buzz.*

5. *Left above. Bubbly!*, a Charlot 'Musical
Entertainment' by John Hastings Turner.
Comedy Theatre, 1917. A stock dramatic
situation as it would be played by the Stage
Society and titled *Muck*. Three other styles
were also parodied by Jack Hulbert, Arthur
Playfair, Winnie Melville and Laura Cowie.

6. *Left.* Teddie Gerard and chorus in *Bubbly!*
sing 'She'd a hole in her stocking' by Austin
Melford and Philip Braham.

70. *Above. Tails Up!* by John Hastings Turner. Comedy Theatre, 1918. Jack Buchanan and Phyllis Monkman sing 'Any little thing' by Ivor Novello.

71. *Below. As You Were* by Arthur Wimperis. Cochran's 'Fantastic Revue'. London Pavilion, 1918. Alice Delysia as Lucifer in 'The Morality Play' scene, wearing the much discussed Paul Poiret costume.

'Down! Evil spirits! On your faces fall
For here comes Lucifer—a match for all.'

72. *Above.* The *Whirligig* by Albert de Courville, Wal Pink and Edgar Wallace. Palace Theatre, 1919. 'The Temple of Chance' with the Palace Girls as the Games of Chance, presided over by Mabel Twemlow as the Goddess.

73. *Right.* Violet Loraine in *The New Whirligig*, 1920. She took over in the second edition of *The Whirligig* which had been produced at the Palace Theatre the previous year. Among her songs were: 'A gipsy warned me', 'The Japanese Sandman' and 'Oh by Jingo! Oh by Gee!'.

74. *Above. Joy-Bells!*, de Courville's ninth revue. London Hippodrome, 1919.

'One of the most beautiful scenes is the spring setting into which "A Winter Fantasy" is transformed, and in which Miss Phyllis Bedells and the chorus perform a most graceful dance intended to symbolise the opening of the spring and the coming of the flowers.'

75. *Below. Splinters*. Savoy Theatre, 1919. Reg Stone, Eliot Makeham and Company,

'An outstanding feature of the organisation is the talented *corps de ballet* composed of soldiers who have seen service in the trenches.'

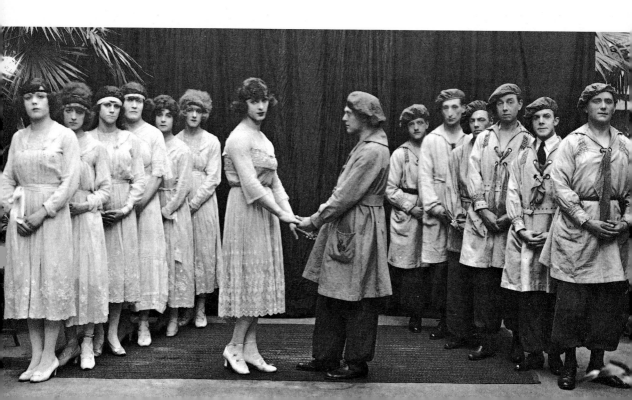

76. *Left. Jumble Sale* by John Hastings Turner. Vaudeville Theatre, 1920. 'Binnie Hale 'the brilliant young daughter of Robert Hale, the famous comedian, is making a big success. Amongst her best efforts are imitations of well known actors and actresses. She is absolutely priceless as her own father, in his rôle of Madame Lucy, the man-milliner, in *Irene*.'

77. *Right.* Binnie Hale in the same Charlot revue. 'When she comes on as Phyllis Monkman, one could almost swear that the popular dancer herself had appeared.'

78. *Above. League of Notions* by John Murray Anderson and Augustus Barratt. New Oxford Theatre, 1921. 'On the 'Alls', George Hassell, A. W. Baskcomb, Rosie and Jennie Dolly and Clifford Morgan.

    'Now let me just show how the turns used to go
    On the Music 'Alls of long, long ago.'

79. *Below.* 'The Bridal Veil' in Cochran's *League of Notions*. The Dolly Sisters as the bride and bridesmaid of the future in Paul Poiret dresses, parade while Josephine Trix sings:

    'Worn in every generation by some happy bride,
    How many hearts you have thrilled—what hope
                you have wakened and filled
    My bridal veil!'

80. *Left*. Gwen Farrar and Norah Blaney in *Pot Luck!*, a Charlot 'Cabaret Show'. Vaudeville Theatre, 1921. A vaudeville act 'About a Piano'.

'Gwen Farrar's performance as a 'cellist, with Norah Blaney as a pianist, is one of the cleverest and smartest on the music-hall stage, as in addition to its musical excellence, the repartee and back chat which go on are very amusing.'

81. *Right*. Dorothy Dickson and Carl Hyson in *London, Paris and New York*. London Pavilion, 1921. The dance team imported by Cochran from New York for the second edition of the revue to make their London debut.

82. *Above. The Co-optimists* in 'A Midsummer Night's Scream', a Pierrotic entertainment. Royalty Theatre, 1921.
The original company:—Stanley Holloway, Melville Gideon, Davy Burnaby, Laddie Cliff, Gilbert Childs, H. B. Hedley, Betty Chester, Phyllis Monkman, Elsa Macfarlane and Babs Valerie.

83. *Left*. Laddie Cliff and Phyllis Monkman sing 'We'll go to church on Sunday', a Melville Gideon song in an early edition of *The Co-optimists*.

The original show was written by Davy Burnaby, Laddie Cliff and Archibald de Bear, with music by Melville Gideon and directed by Laddie Cliff. Many contributions by other authors and composers, including Noël Coward, were used in the subsequent six editions of the original run, which lasted till 1927.

84. *Below*. Betty Chester in 'The Bandsman's Daughter', with Davy Burnaby, Gilbert Childs, Laddie Cliff and Stanley Holloway.

85. *Left. Fun of the Fayre* by John Hastings Turner and Augustus Barratt. London Pavilion, 1921.
The Dolly Sisters, while playing at the New Oxford Theatre in *League of Notions*, slipped into another Cochran revue to dance a Pony Dance with Clifton Webb.

86. *Below. Fun of the Fayre.* The 'Hurlingham' scene—opening chorus 'Polo'—with Clifton Webb, June, Walter Williams, Evelyn Laye, Joan Clarkson, Albert Bruno and Juliette Compton.

87. *Above left.* Stanley Lupino as Dan Leno in *The Peep-Show*, a revue by Lauri Wylie and James W. Tate. London Hippodrome, 1921. 'The Song Shop'—Reminiscence of the Old Time Song'.

88. *Above right. Rockets.* London Palladium, 1922. Lorna and Toots Pounds with Charles Austin sing the 'Klaxon Horn Jazz' in Harry Day's 'Super-Revue'. Devised and staged by Charles Henry.

89. *Below. Mayfair and Montmarte* by John Hastings Turner. New Oxford Theatre, 1922. A lavish Cochran production with a ballet, 'A legend of the Sun Worshipper of old Peru'. Scene, dresses and ballet arranged by Stowitts, with himself as the Lover, George Bishop as the Inca King and Delysia as the King's daughter (dedicated as a sacrifice to the Sun).

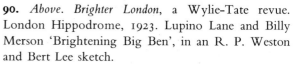

90. *Above. Brighter London*, a Wylie-Tate revue. London Hippodrome, 1923. Lupino Lane and Billy Merson 'Brightening Big Ben', in an R. P. Weston and Bert Lee sketch.

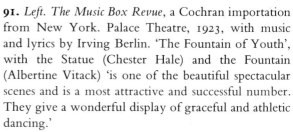

91. *Left. The Music Box Revue*, a Cochran importation from New York. Palace Theatre, 1923, with music and lyrics by Irving Berlin. 'The Fountain of Youth', with the Statue (Chester Hale) and the Fountain (Albertine Vitack) 'is one of the beautiful spectacular scenes and is a most attractive and successful number. They give a wonderful display of graceful and athletic dancing.'

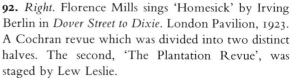

92. *Right.* Florence Mills sings 'Homesick' by Irving Berlin in *Dover Street to Dixie*. London Pavilion, 1923. A Cochran revue which was divided into two distinct halves. The second, 'The Plantation Revue', was staged by Lew Leslie.

93. *Above. London Calling*, a Charlot revue. Duke of York's Theatre, 1923. The book was a collaboration of Noël Coward and Ronald Jeans, while all the lyrics and music were by Coward.

'The Swiss Family Whittlebot' with Tubby Edlin introducing Leonard Childs as Gob, William Childs as Sago and Maisie Gay as Hernia Whittlebot, in the burlesque of the Sitwells of which Coward says:

'During the first two weeks of the run, I received to my intense surprise, a cross letter from Osbert Sitwell—in fact, so angry was it, that I first of all imagined it to be a joke. However, it was far from being a joke, and shortly afterwards another letter arrived, even crosser than the first. To this day I am still a little puzzled as to why that light-hearted burlesque should have aroused him, his brother, and his sister to such paroxysms of fury. But the fact remains that it did, and I believe still does.'

94. *Below*. Noël Coward and chorus singing 'Other girls'. Coward, Gertrude Lawrence and Maisie Gay were the stars of the revue.

95. *Right.* Gertrude Lawrence in the Coward sketch 'Early Mourning'.

'Miss Poppy Baker is rung up in the morning and told that her husband has just committed suicide by jumping off Waterloo Bridge. Though secretly rather pleased than otherwise, she rings up all her friends, pretending to be in a dreadful frame of mind, and makes appointments with them at Ciro's. Presently, however, she discovers that a mistake has been made, and that the "bad news" concerns the people in the flat above. Then the curtain comes down, and the flow of Poppy Baker's language is mercifully "cut off".'

96. *Right.* Gertrude Lawrence singing 'Parisian Pierrot' as a boudoir doll, designed by Edward Molyneux.

97. Cicely Courtneidge and Jack Hulbert as 'The two Freshers' in *The Little Revue Starts at Nine*. Little Theatre, 1923. Edward Laurillard's intimate revue directed by Jack Hulbert with songs and sketches by numerous authors.

98. *Right.* Hermione Baddeley and Sonnie Hale sing 'Chilli-Bom-Bom' by Cliff Friend and Walter Donaldson in *The Punch Bowl*. Archibald de Bear's revue, Duke of York's Theatre, 1924.

99. *Below. Puppets!.* Vaudeville Theatre, 1924. ' "A musical interlude", an amusing burlesque without words, devised by Stanley Lupino and made possible by the help of Binnie Hale.'

100. *Left. Charlot's Revue* opened at the Prince of Wales' Theatre in September, 1924, and ran into numerous editions, with monthly changes of material and cast, until 1926 and was to be followed later by *The Charlot Show of 1926* at the same theatre, eventually to tour as *Charlot's Repertoire Revue.* In January 1924 he took a company to New York as *André Charlot's London Revue of 1924.* Much of the material had been taken from previous successes, and later both its stars and numbers were seen in London at the Prince of Wales'. His next American revue was introduced to London in 1925 before going to New York. Gertrude Lawrence sang 'Limehouse Blues' by Philip Braham both in New York and London.

101. *Below.* 'In Fools Paradise', the finale of the first *Charlot's Revue.* Dorothy Dolman, Hugh Sinclair, Dorothy Debenham, William Senior, Queenie Thomas, Henry Kendall, Phyllis Monkman, Maisie Gay, Morris Harvey, Juliette Compton, Peter Haddon, Kitty Attfield, Leonard Henry and Nellie Bowman.

102. *Left.* 'Tea Shop Tattle', a sketch by Dion Titheradge. *Charlot's Revue*, 1925 'As played in America'. Beatrice Lillie as Gwladys and Herbert Mundin as Second man.

103. *Below.* Beatrice Lillie and chorus sing 'March with me', by Douglas Furber and Ivor Novello.

104. *Left.* Gertrude Lawrence and Beatrice Lillie in 'Fallen Babies', a skit on *Fallen Angels* by Ronald Jeans and Ivor Novello in *Charlot's Revue*.

'The two bottles containing gin instead of the more usual milk are placed in the babies' mouths, with the result that they get thoroughly "tight", in the same way as the two "angels" in Mr Noël Coward's play!'

105. *Right.* Gertrude Lawrence and Jack Buchanan sing 'No-one's ever kissed me', by Ronald Jeans and Philip Braham.

106. *Above*. Beatrice Lillie as Madame Wanda Allova, supported by Hazel Wynne as Monsieur Toldoff in 'Sealed Feet', 'A Romantic Reverie in One Act', a burlesque Russian ballet by Quentin Tod, to music by Charles Prentice. The *corps de ballet* were called: Mesdames Bitova, Hangova, Halfseezova, Riteova, Cumova, Pastova, Pullova, Shottova, Turnova, Leanova, Beenova, Fallova, Wellova, Tideova, Thrownova.

107. *Below*. 'The Masque of Millamant' after Aubrey Beardsley, a ballet by Quentin Tod with music by Ivor Novello. Dorothy Dickson as Millamant and Quentin Tod as Cosme (her coiffeur).

108. *Above. On with the Dance*, Cochran's London Pavilion Revue, 1925. The book and lyrics by Noël Coward and music by Philip Braham and Noël Coward. The ballet 'The Rake', 'A Hogarth Impression', was by Leonide Massine with music by Roger Quilter. The Beau and the Corset-woman—Massine and Eleanora Marra.

109. *Left.* Alice Delysia sings Coward's 'Cosmopolitan Lady' in a Jean Patou creation in *On with the Dance.*

110. *Above* 'Fête Galante' (a Vicarage Garden Party). Hermione Baddeley as Nellie sings 'The Vicarage Dance', a Coward *jeu d'esprit*,

'I'm just seventeen and a rogue of a girl
My heart is throbbing with carnival's whirl.'

111. *Below*. 'Oranges and Lemons' by Noël Coward. Douglas Byng as Grace Hubbard and Ernest Thesiger as Violet Banks. 'Please, please allow me . . . I'm used to Venetians, we had them in our house at Boulogne when I was a girl.'

112. *Left*. *Sky High*. London Palladium, 1925. 'Y[...] lips say "yes",' sung by 'Jack Dewar and October[...] Arthur Riscoe and Nellie Wallace give a burles[...] of Jack Buchanan and June in a de Courville rev[...]

113. *Below*. *By the Way*. Apollo Theatre, 1[...] 'Cleansing the stage', a burlesque by Harold Simp[...] of *Spring Cleaning* by Frederick Lonsdale, w[...] Cicely Courtneidge, Charles Courtneidge, J[...] Hulbert, Marie Arnold, April Harmon, Ha[...] French and Winnie Meyern, in the second edition[...]

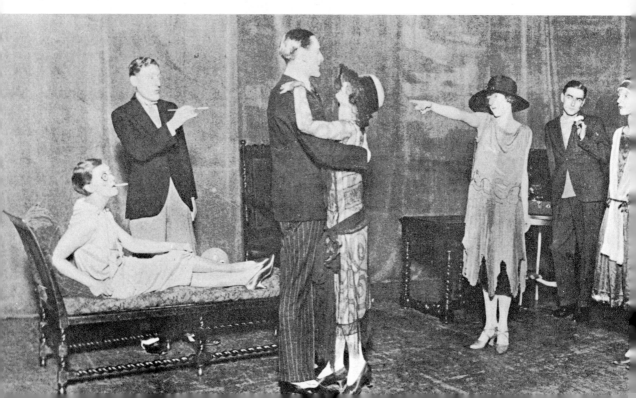

114. *Above. Blackbirds*, Cochran's importation of Lew Leslie's coloured revue. London Pavilion, 1926. The finale of the first half led by Florence Mills.

115. *Below. Tricks*. Apollo Theatre, 1925. 'Diaghileff Re-chauvé', a burlesque by Harold Simpson of the current Russian ballet and Chauve-souris craze, with music by Helen Trix and Les Copeland, with Marjorie Robertson (Anna Neagle), Wilbur Lenton, Arthur Chesney and Margaret Yarde.

116. *Left.* Spinelly in *Cochran's Revue* (*1926*) by Ronald Jeans. London Pavilion.

117. *Below. R.S.V.P.* Archibald de Bear's revue. Vaudeville Theatre, 1926. Cyril Ritchard with Joyce Barbour, Mimi Crawford and Enid Stamp-Taylor in the opening number by Jack Strachey.

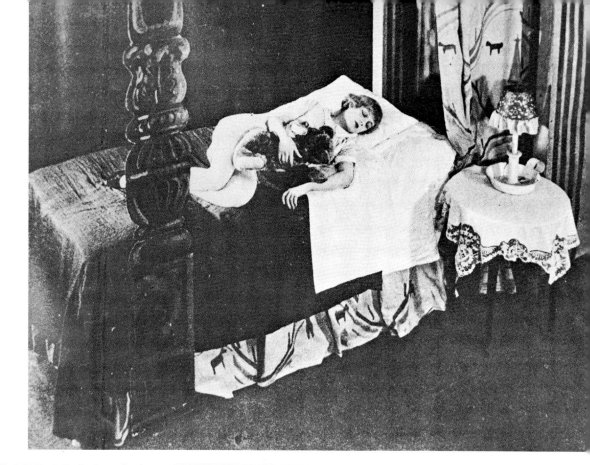

Above. R.S.V.P. Mimi Crawford as [Chris]topher Robin in 'When we were very [youn]g', sings the songs of A. A. Milne with [Fr]aser-Simson's music.

Right. Jessie Matthews in *The Charlot [Revue] of 1926*, Prince of Wales' Theatre, [light]ens up Grand Guignol with a Richard [Rus]sell song in 'Making playgoing [saf]er'.

120. *Right. One Dam Thing After Another,* Cochran's London Pavilion revue 1927, by Ronald Jeans, lyrics by Lorenz Hart and music by Richard Rodgers. Edythe Baker, at her white piano, plays 'The Birth of the Blues', by Ray Henderson. 'The brilliant jazz-pianist, whose success is not by any means confined to her instrumental fireworks. A song and dance is performed with the same easy confidence as the most involved efforts in pianoforte syncopation.'

121. *Left.* The '7th Dam Thing', Ric[h] Dolman and Jessie Matthews sing heart stood still', 'while the two little pec[ple] Brian Glennis and Gwen Stella, mak[e] charming addition to the dance follows.'

> 'I took one look at you
> That's all I meant to do
> And then my heart stood still.'

122. *Above. Clowns in Clover* by Ronald Jeans with music by Noel Gay. Adelphi Theatre, 1927. June, Jack Hulbert, Cicely Courtneidge, Bobbie Comber and Irene Russell. 'Clowns at play' the finale to the first half.

123. *Right.* 'The Great White Sale' by Dion Titheradge. Cicely Courtneidge as Mrs Spooner in the Linen Department of Harridge's attempts to order—two dozen double damask dinner napkins from Ivor McLaren and Bobbie Comber, in the second edition of *Clowns in Clover*, 1928. Directed by Jack Hulbert.

124. *Above. This Year of Grace.* London Pavilion, 1928, with book, lyrics and music by Noël Coward. Jessie Matthews sings 'Teach me to dance like Grandma', with Mr Cochran's Young Ladies—Nancy Barnett, Madeline Gibson, Marjorie Browne, Peter May, Florita Fey, Marjorie Robertson (Anna Neagle), Peggy Wynne and Greta Taylor.

125. *Below.* 'Dance, Little Lady' Lauri Devine and the dancers in Oliver Messel masks and dresses.

126. *Right*. 'A Room with a View.' Jessie Matthews and Sonnie Hale in a Marc Henri and Laverdet setting.

127. *Below*. 'Law and Order'. Policewoman Pellet (Douglas Byng) and Policewoman Wendle (Maisie Gay) gossip while violence is committed.

128. *Left.* Gracie Fields in *The Show's the Thing*, an Archie Pitt revue at the Victoria Palace, 1929, which later transferred to the Lyceum Theatre.

Gracie Fields came to London in touring revues, first at the Middlesex Music Hall in 1915 and later at the Alhambra Theatre in *Mr Tower of London* in 1923.

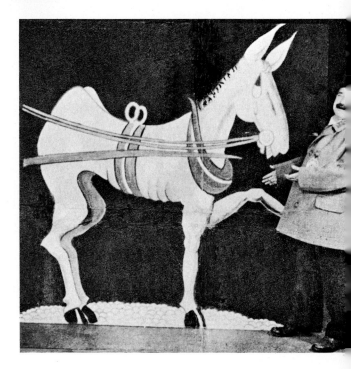

129. *Right.* Billy Bennett in *Coo-ee*. Vaudeville Theatre, 1929. The London Cabby with a horse, designed by Aubrey Hammond.

130. *Above. The House That Jack Built.* Adelphi Theatre, 1929.
'The Dowager Fairy Queen', a Pantomime burlesque by Douglas Furber and Ivor Novello. The Principal Boy (Joan McLaren), The Fairy Queen (Cicely Courtneidge), the Principal Girl (Rosaline Corneille), the Demon King (Stuart Harding) and the Witch (Elinor Darville).

131. *Below left.* 'The Ever Open Door' by Ronald Jeans. Cicely Courtneidge and Jack Hulbert as Rose and Henry Carroway 'settling the knick-knacks at the semi-detached villa in Harringay'.

132. *Below right.* 'And the Next' by Ronald Jeans. Cicely Courtneidge as the 'naice' Miss Parfitt, the Postmistress at Branchaven, on the look out for a young man.

133. *Above. Charles B. Cochran's 1930 Revue.*
London Pavilion. By Beverley Nichols and Vivian
Ellis. Mr Cochran's Young Ladies—dressed by Reville
—Ada Fay, Peggy Cartwright, Sepha Treble, Dolly
King, Trixie Scales, Sheila Wilson, Peggy Willoughby,
Sara Smith, Peggy Rawlings, Olive Melville, Dorothy
Dobson, Gladys Lincoln, Dorothy Jackson, Peggy
Beaty, Aimee Gillespie, Kathleen Gibson.

134. *Below left.* 'Luna Park', or 'The Freaks'. A ball
by Boris Kochno with music by Lord Berners an
choreography by George Balanchine, with Serg
Lifar, Alice Nikitina, Richard Domonsky ar
Constantin Tcherkas.

135. *Below right.* Ada May—'Lighter than air'. Th
ubiquitous 'Balloon Dance'.

136. *Right. De La Folie Pure.*
Victoria Palace, 1930. 'Une Romance de Vienne' with Max Turgan-
off and Elaine Lettor as the Singers
and Marika Rökk as Dancer—'the
charm of the eighteenth century is
evoked by costume and melody'—
straight from the Folies Bergère.

137. *Below right. The Chelsea
Follies*, an Archie de Bear revue.
Victoria Palace, 1930. Jimmy
Nervo and Teddy Knox in 'The
Chelsea Flower Show' dance with
Peggy Cartwright and Toni Grecco
—straight from the King's Road!

138. *Left*. *Charlot's Masquerade* by Ronald Jea
and Rowland Leigh. Cambridge Theatre, 193
The opening production of a new theatre.
'The Masque of the Red Death', a ballet b
Quentin Tod, with music by Cyril Scott. Do
Vadimova and Anton Dolin as Medusa an
Perseus with Quentin Tod as the Jester.

139. *Below*. Patrick Waddington and Constan
Carpenter sing 'I fell for you' by William Walke

140. *Above.* Henry Kendall, J. H. Roberts and Reginald Smith as Edgar Wallace, Hannen Swaffer and Charles B. Cochran, three distinguished guests, in the finale to the first half.

141. *Right.* 'Counter Attractions' by Ronald Jeans. Henry Kendall (Horace Bittars), Beatrice Lillie (Miss Bleet) and Florence Desmond (Miss Cannop), in 'Miss Bleet's General Store in a country village'.

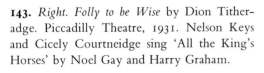

142. *Left. Walk This Way!*, an Archie Pitt revue. Winter Garden Theatre, 1931. Gracie Fields as Queen of the Pearlies sings 'Cockney Jazz' in 'Way down East'.

143. *Right. Folly to be Wise* by Dion Titheradge. Piccadilly Theatre, 1931. Nelson Keys and Cicely Courtneidge sing 'All the King's Horses' by Noel Gay and Harry Graham.

144. *Right. Revudeville* Number 32. Windmill Theatre, 1933.
'Fountain of Youth'—Elsie Tower, Bobbie Bradshaw and Diana Vawser.
'This is one of the Tableaux considered by the majority of our patrons to be the most beautiful which have yet been staged in this House which is noted for its beautiful Tableaux.'

145. *Below. Revudeville* Number 228. Windmill Theatre, 1950.
'Death comes to the Infanta', Reg Drew, Christine Welsford, Mellonie Whymark, Vanessa Terry, Jobyna Millhouse and Keith Lester.
'We never closed'—they never clothed—and they never changed!

146. *Above. Bow Bells*, a John Murray Anderson revue. London Hippodrome, 1932. 'Love keeps out of the rain', a production number, sung by Lance Fairfax and Joan Gardner, and danced by Harold Turner and Ruth Mackand ('Rainy Weather') and Delsya and Freddie Carpenter ('Fair Weather'), to choreography by Ninette de Valois. In the *corps de ballet* are Jean Gillie and Sally Gray (Connie Stevens), two future stars.

147. *Left* Robert Hale and Binnie Hale as the old and the new Dick Whittington 'Discuss the merits of past and present' in a Dion Titheradge sketch, 'Turn Again'.

148. *Right. Oxford Blazers*, 'The Undergraduate Follies'. Little Theatre, 1932. John Glyn-Jones, Diana Lincoln, Christopher Hassall, Margery Binner, Desmond Davis, Elaine Lettor, Giles Playfair, Audrey Cameron and Anthony Spurgin. Giles Playfair's revue with book by Aubrey C. Ensor and Arthur Watkyn and music by Anthony Spurgin and Michael Sayer. Directed by Stephen Thomas.

149. *Below. Savoy Follies*, Archie de Bear's revue. Savoy Theatre, 1932. 'Days of the old Savoy' with Gillie Potter (Sentry), John Mack (Marco), Florence Desmond (Mrs Cripps), Stanley Holloway (The Singer), Hal Bryan (Jack Point), Rita Mackay (Mabel), Iris Ashley, Polly Ward and Bertha Riccardo (The Three Little Maids).

150. *Above. Words and Music* by Noël Coward.
Adelphi Theatre, 1932.
Ivy St Helier as Lady Mullenty and Gerald Nodin as
Sir Ronald Mullenty relax while Romney Brent
as The Reverend Inigo Banks sings 'Mad dogs and
Englishmen'. First sung by Beatrice Lillie in *The
Third Little Show*, New York, 1931.

151. *Left.* 'Children's Hour'. Steffi Duna, Doris
Hare and John Mills as Lilli, Jane and Bobby sing
'Let's Live Dangerously' in *Words and Music*.

152. *Above. How D'You Do?*, Charlot's revue. Comedy Theatre, 1933.
'Exposures' by Arthur Macrae gives a glimpse of ancient Rome, with Frances Day as Poppea, Edward Chapman as Nero and Douglas Byng as Boadicea—'Queen of the Obsceni'. 'O, those ru-id Druids'.

153. *Right. Please*, Charlot's revue. Savoy Theatre, 1933.
Beatrice Lillie as Frisco Fanny and Lupino Lane as Klondike in a Robert Macgunigle sketch with Henry Sullivan's music.

154. *Above.* Douglas Byng sings 'Miss Otis regrets' by Cole Porter in *Hi Diddle Diddle!*, Comedy Theatre, 1934. Miss Otis' portrait by Clark Hutton.

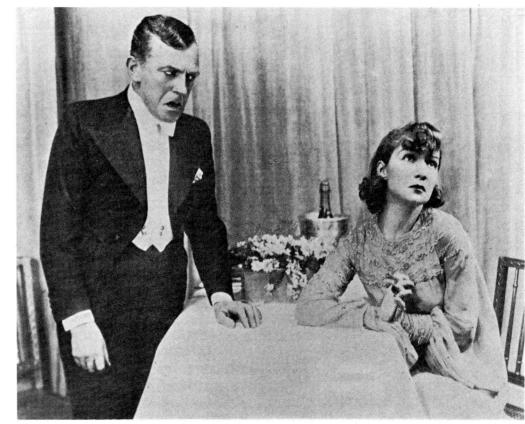

Above. Why Not To-night?. Palace Theatre, 1934.
son Keys and Florence Desmond indulge in an
–Star Breakfast', and 'relieve that "breakfast when
're married" feeling by impersonating film stars
ı brilliant rapidity! Desmond is doing a "Christina"
ıment of Greta Garbo's, while "Bunch" Keys as
don Harker butts in on her rhapsodies.'

159. *Above. Stop Press* b
Newman, with music a
Directed by Hassard Sh
'Here's to the Noël Cow
one day he find greatnt
toast in the sketch enti
Playwright, Leaves New

156. *Below. Streamline*, Cochran's revue. Palace
Theatre, 1934.
' "Perseverance" (by Turbot and Vulligan)', A. P.
Herbert's burlesque of a Gilbert and Sullivan Opera,
with music by Vivian Ellis. Florence Desmond as
Perseverance, with Charles Heslop, Naunton Wayne
and Esmond Knight, assisted by Fisher Girls and
Bailiffs sort out a knotty 'Gilbertian' problem.

161. *Above. Encore les Dames.* Prince of Wales' Theatre, 1936.
Freedom for '*Les Oiseaux Prisonniers*' at Alfred Esdaile's 'London's Folies Bergère'.

162. *Left. Spread it Abroad* by Herbert Farjeon, with music by William Walker. Saville Theatre, 1936.
Ivy St Helier and Nelson Keys as two temperamental operatic stars have a 'Re-union in Covent Garden'.

158. *Right.* Flore[...]
on a 'New Reco[...]
Potts, the first [...]
Pole with her ba[...]

163. *Above left. Follow the Sun*, 'Charles B. Cochran's 1936 Revue'. Adelphi Theatre. 'Cruising; or, "English as she is spoke"' by Ronald Jeans with Claire Luce (an American Girl), Frank Pettingell (a Deck Steward), Ada Reeve (a Lancashire Wife) and Nick Long Jnr (an American).

164. *Above.* 'The First Shoot', a ballet by Osbert Sitwell, with music by William Walton and choreography by Frederick Ashton in a Cecil Beaton décor. Claire Luce as Lady de Fontenoy (formerly Connie Winsome of the Gaiety or Daly's) and Nick Long Jnr as Lord Charles Canterbury.

165. *Below left. Home and Beauty*, 'Cochran's Coronation Revue' by A. P. Herbert. Adelphi Theatre, 1937. Nelson Keys and Binnie Hale, as the Plumber and Annie, sing the praises of 'A nice cup of tea' in Henry Sullivan's song.

166. *Above. London Rhapsody*, George Black's London Palladium revue, 1937. Sub-titled 'A Symphony of a great City'—The Crazy Gang: Chesney Allen, Charlie Naughton, Teddy Knox, Bud Flanagan, Jimmy Gold and Jimmy Nervo, sing 'Six Broken Blossoms' by Bert Lee and Harris Weston 'In the Shadow of Eros—Piccadilly'.

167. *Below. Nine Sharp*, Herbert Farjeon's Little Theatre revue 1938, with Walter Leigh's music. 'Heavenly Bodies', Hermione Baddeley and Cyril Ritchard—'I do love the stars—which are Nervo and Knox?'

168. *Left. Herbert Farjeon's Little Revue*, Little Theatre, 1939.
Hermione Baddeley as Mlle Allova and Cyril Ritchard as Harold Helpmeet dance 'The Creaking Princess' to Walter Leigh's music. Designed and directed by Hedley Briggs.

169. *Below. The Gate Revue*. Ambassadors Theatre, 1939. By Diana Morgan and Robert MacDermot with music by Geoffrey Wright. Norman Marshall's production from the Gate Theatre.
'Tatler Time', the opening of the second half with Gabrielle Brune, Michael Wilding, Hermione Gingold, Walter Crisham, Doris Gilmore and Jack McNaughton.

170. *Top left. Shephard's Pie*, Firth Shephard's 'menu of song, dance and laughter', by Douglas Furber. Princes Theatre, 1939. Arthur Riscoe, Sydney Howard and Richard Hearne—'Seeing Life'.

171. *Top right. Black Velvet*, 'George Black's New Intimate Rag'. Directed by Robert Nesbitt. London Hippodrome, 1939. Roma Beaumont and Vic Oliver entertain.

172. *Below.* 'My heart belongs to Daddy' by Cole Porter. 'The Gold-Diggers of 1939'. Roberta Huby, Pat Kirkwood, Carole Lynne and Norma Dawn costumed in fox by Norman Hartnell.

173. *Right. All Clear.* Queen's Theatre, 1939. An H. M. Tennent revue with contributions by many hands. Directed by Harold French.
Bobbie Howes and Beatrice Lillie as Miss Lilian Mawdsley and Miss Eva Tassel in Noël Coward's 'Cat's Cradle', originally seen in New York in *The Third Little Show*, 1931.
'I suppose you 'aven't seen my Minnie anywhere, 'ave you?' 'Your what, Miss Mawdsley?' 'My Minnie—my cat.'

174. *Above left*. Evelyn Laye sings 'Only a glass o
champagne' by Arthur Wimperis and Noel Gay i.
Lights Up! 'Cochran's 1940 Revue', Savoy Theatre.

175. *Above right*. Patricia Burke as the Cigarette Gir
in the night-club scene 'Chez Henson' in Firt
Shephard's *Up and Doing*, Saville Theatre, 1940.

176. *Left*. Judy Campbell sings 'A nightingale sang i
Berkeley Square' by Eric Maschwitz and Mannin
Sherwin, in *New Faces*. Comedy Theatre, 1940.

177. *Above left.* *Up and Doing.* Leslie Henson and Stanley Holloway, under the Fougasse poster, warn against 'Careless Talk' in a Graham John sketch.

178. *Above right.* *Up and Doing.* Binnie Hale and Cyril Ritchard burlesque two fan dancers in the night-club scene, which included numbers by Rodgers and Hart originally in *The Boy from Syracuse.*

179. *Right. Fun and Games.* Princes Theatre, 1941. Firth Shephard's 'A New Show of Song, Dance and Laughter' by Douglas Furber. It included 'The Royal Raviolis', 'The world's most wonderful equilibrists, appearing for the first time in this country, Vera Pearce, Phil Trix, Sydney Howard, Arthur Riscoe, Bobby Rudd and Richard Hearne in very effective disguise.'

180. *Above left. Rise Above It* by Leslie Julian Jones with numerous other contributors. Comedy Theatre, 1941. Hermione Baddeley and Hermione Gingold together for the first time in 'Under Their Hats' by Denis Waldock.

181. *Above right. Diversion.* Wyndham's Theatre, 194 A Bronson Albery 'blitz' time afternoon all-st mixture. Devised by Herbert Farjeon. Edith Evans the 'Hop-picker'.

182. *Below left. Diversion No. 2* 1941.
'In for a Dip' by Harold Purcell and George Posford. The bathing belles, Vida Hope and Joan Sterndale Bennett, were assisted by Peter Ustinov and Derek Bogerde (Dirk Bogarde).

183. *Below right. Strike It Again.* George Blac revue, Prince of Wales' Theatre, 1944.
Sid Field in 'Portrait Study' by Martin Lane.
'Show me your teeth—no, don't take them out.'

184. *Above. Hi-Diddle-Diddle.* On tour 1942. Jane, the Daily Mirror girl, and Al Marshall. A war-time strip revue.

185. *Below. Best Bib and Tucker,* George Black's London Palladium revue, 1942. Tommy Trinder as Carmen Miranda sings 'No, No, No, No, Columbus' by Val Guest, assisted by Edmundo Ros and his band.

186. *Left. Sweet and Low.* Ambassadors Theatre, 1943.
Walter Crisham and Hermione Gingold discuss the stars in 'Poison Ivy' by Denis Waldock.

187. *Below left. Sweeter and Lower.* Ambassadors Theatre, 1944.
Hermione Gingold as Charmaine 'For services rendered' by Alan Melville.

188. *Below right. Sweetest and Lowest.* Ambassadors Theatre, 1946.
Henry Kendall and Hermione Gingold. The three revues, directed by Charles Hickman, covered the years from 1943 to 1947, becoming an institution and making the names of Alan Melville and Charles Zwar.

189. *Above left. Sigh no More*, written, composed and directed by Noël Coward. Piccadilly Theatre, 1945.
Graham Payn sings 'Matelot' in a G. E. Calthrop setting.

190. *Above right.* Joyce Grenfell sings her own song 'Du Maurier' with Richard Addinsell's music.

191. *Below.* Cyril Ritchard, Madge Elliott, Joyce Grenfell and Graham Payn as 'The Burchells of Battersea Rise'.

192. *Above. Tuppence Coloured*, Laurier Lister's revue for the Company of Four. Lyric Theatre, Hammersmith, 1947. (Later transferred to the Globe Theatre.) Max Adrian as the eccentric signalman 'Between the lines' by Nicholas Phipps and Geoffrey Wright in an Emett décor.

193. *Below left. Oranges and Lemons*, Laurier Lister's revue for the Company of Four. Lyric Theatre, Hammersmith, 1948. (Later transferred to the Globe Theatre.) Silvia Ashmole and Denis Martin sing 'Someday' by Joyce Grenfell and Richard Addinsell.

194. *Below right.* Elisabeth Welch, Max Adrian and Diana Churchill close the first half with ' . . . . food of love' by Nicholas Phipps and Geoffrey Wright.

95. *Above. A La Carte.* Firth Shepherd's Savoy Theatre revue, 1948, by a well tried team, Alan Melville and Charles Zwar, with décor, dresses and dances by William Chappell under the direction of Norman Marshall.

'he closing of the first half, 'Labour's Lost Love', 'is delightfully imaginative in solving political problems. The Prime Minister (Michael Anthony) and Leader of the Opposition (Gordon Bell) of this state strike a familiar note. Henry Kendall as Justice and Hermione Baddeley as Love lend a big hand in smoothing things out, with the assistance of Nigel Neilson and Dick Henderson, Jnr.'

196. *Below. Slings and Arrows.* Comedy Theatre, 1948. A revue devised by Hermione Gingold and Charles Hickman. The first half ends with 'Bless the Show' by Leslie Julian Jones, a burlesque on Cochran's *Bless the Bride*, with Hermione Gingold, Walter Crisham, Gretchen Franklin and the Company

'And we were delighted
When Father was knighted,
So Bless the Show!'

197. *Above. Penny Plain*, a Laurier Lister revue. St Martin's Theatre, 1951.
Rose Hill, Joyce Grenfell and Moyra Fraser make 'Joyful Noise' by Joyce Grenfell and Donald Swann in Osbert Lancaster's version of the Albert Hall.

198. *Below. The Lyric Revue*. Lyric Theatre, Hammersmith, 1951. (Transferred later to the Globe Theatre.) 'Let's ignore it', the opening number by Gerard Bryant and Charles Zwar. Directed by William Chappell with Roberta Huby, Ian Carmichael, Joan Heal, Jeremy Hawk, Irlin Hall, Myles Eason, Dora Bryan, Graham Payn, Hilary Allen, George Benson, Pam Marmont and Tommy Linden.

199. *Globe Revue.* Globe Theatre, 1952. Yet another in the famous Company of Four and H. M. Tennent series. Directed by William Chappell with Loudon Sainthill's décor and contributions by many hands. Dora Bryan, Graham Payn, Joan Heal and Ian Carmichael sing Noël Coward's 'Bad times are just around the corner'.

200. *Above. Excitement.* London Casino, 1951.
One of a series of 'Latin Quarter' revues staged by
Robert Nesbitt for Tom Arnold and Emile Littler
between 1949 and 1952. West-end sophistication.

201. *Below. Soir de Paris* on the road 1952. Touring
exoticism.

202. *Above left. Airs on a Shoestring.* Laurier Lister's revue. Royal Court Theatre, 1953.
Directed by Alfred Rodrigues with contributions by many hands. Max Adrian and Moyra Fraser in 'Taken as Red', a satire on *Hiawatha* at the Albert Hall, by David Climie and John Pritchett.

203. *Above right.* 'Sing High, Sing Low', a burlesque by Madeleine Dring of the eternal romantic duettists, by Betty Marsden and Jack Gray
'How we sang 'til we hadn't the strength to encore.'

204. *Below.* 'Guide to Britten' by Michael Flanders and Donald Swann.
Denis Quilley, Peter Reeves, Max Adrian, Charles Ross and Bernard Hunter in a skit on a famous composer and his operas
'Nor did Uncle Benjy forget the dear little children.'

205. *Above. Intimacy at 8.30.* Criterion Theatre, 1954. A revue by Peter Myers, Alec Grahame and David Climie, with music by John Pritchett and Ronald Cass. Directed by Michael Charnley. A West-end revised version of an earlier New Lindsey Theatre, Notting Hill Gate, production of 1952. 'The Boy Friend's Girl Friend', Eleanor Fazan and *Les Boys*—Digby Wolfe, Ronnie Stevens, Geoffrey Hibbert and Ron Moody in front.

206. *Below. The Punch Revue.* Duke of York's Theatre, 1955. Devised and directed by Vida Hope, written and designed by contributors to Punch. 'London 1841', the opening number in a Joan and David de Bethel setting. The company led by Binnie Hale with Paul Daneman, Joyce Blair, Denis Martin and Alfie Bass.

207. *Above. La Plume de ma Tante.* Garrick Theatre, 1955.
Robert Dhéry's French Intimate Revue, transplanted to London in its original form with great success. With Colette Brosset, Pierre Olaf, Christian Duvaleix, Robert Dhéry and Jacques Legras.

208. *Below. Such is Life.* Adelphi Theatre, 1955.
'Vitality' a Tiller Girls' routine. One of a series of variety revues starring Radio and Television personalities. Presented by Jack Hylton and George and Alfred Black.

209. *Left. Cranks.* St Martin's Theatre 1956. Written and devised by John Cranko, with music by John Addison and décor by John Piper. This surrealistic revue was first seen at the Watergate Theatre and soon transferred to a larger audience. The company of four, Annie Ross, Anthony Newley, Hugh Bryant and Gilbert Vernon, introduced themselves in 'Who's Who'.

210. *Right. For Amusement Only.* Apollo Theatre, 1956. Another Myers-Cass-Pritchett collaboration again directed by Michael Charnley. (It was to be followed later with *For Adults Only* in 1958.)
'The Vagabond Student' sent up amateur light opera with Thelma Ruby as Carena (a princess in disguise), Ron Moody as Franzl (a penniless student) and Hugh Paddick as Baron von Klott (a traitor).

211. *Below. These Foolish Kings.* Victoria Palace, 1956. Act V Scene 1 of Shakespeare's *A Midsummer Night's Dream*—Pyramus (Bud Flanagan), Thisbe (Charlie Naughton), Quince (Teddy Knox), Wall (Eddie Gray), Moon (Jimmy Gold) and Lion (Jimmy Nervo).
One of the series of Crazy Gang revues which ran almost continuously from 1947 to 1962.

212. *Living for Pleasure*. Garrick Theatre, 1958. An H.M. Tennent revue by Arthur Macrae with music by Richard Addinsell. Directed by William Chappell with a Peter Rice décor.
Dora Bryan as Miss Thompson, assisted by Terry Skelton as the Intruder, perform a hilarious parody of *Le Spectre de la Rose* in 'The Wrong Bedroom'.

213. *Left. Share my Lettuce.* Lyric Theatre Hammersmith, 1957. (Later transferred to the Comedy Theatre.)

'A diversion with music', written by Bamber Gascoigne with music by Keith Statham and Patrick Gowers, and designed by Disley Jones. Directed by Eleanor Fazan.

'Party Games' with Philip Gilbert Johnny Greenland, Roderick Cook Kenneth Williams, Maggie Smith Heather Linson, Barbara Evans and Kenneth Mason.

214. *Above left. Pieces of Eight.* Michael Codron's revue by Peter Cook. Apollo Theatre, 1959. 'If Only' with Kenneth Williams and Fenella Fielding.

A second revue, *One Over the Eight,* followed at the Duke of York's Theatre in 1961. Material by Harold Pinter, N.F. Simpson, Lionel Bart and Sandy Wilson was scattered through these revues.

215. *Above right. One to Another.* Lyric Theatre, Hammersmith, 1959. A revue which transferred to the Apollo Theatre and took twenty writers to compile, and included 'The Black and White' by Harold Pinter with Sheila Hancock and Beryl Reid.

216. *Opposite. One to Another.* Beryl Reid 'Amongst the Vases' by Bamber Gascoigne

217. *Above. On the Brighter Side.* Phoenix Theatre, 1961.
Judy Carne, Betty Marsden and Pip Hinton make 'A plea for the Throne' by Peter Myers and Alec Grahame to music by John Pritchett
    'Where the Hades is the Ladies in the Lords?'

218. *Below. Beyond the Fringe.* Fortune Theatre, 1961. Jonathan Miller, Peter Cook, Alan Bennett and Dudley Moore in the Shakespearean burlesque 'So that's the way you like it' by Jonathan Miller,
    'Now is steel'twixt gut and bladder interposed.'

219. *Above. All Square.* Vaudeville Theatre, 1963.
Written by Alan Melville, music by Charles Zwar
and directed by Charles Hickman.
Led by Beryl Reid and Naunton Wayne the Company walk down—Nicky Henson, Anna Dawson,
John Warner, Joyanne Delancey, Robin Hunter,
Joyce Blair, Robin Palmer, Karen Clare, Julian
Holloway and Jane Murdoch.

220. *Below. Six of One.* Adelphi Theatre, 1963.
Peter Bridge's revue, devised by Francis Essex and
directed by William Chappell, on the stage career
of Dora Bryan. The Concert Party episode, 'The
Sea Stars' by John Taylor, with John Hewer (the
Comic), Amanda Barrie (the Soubrette), Dennis
Lotis (the Singer), Dora Bryan (the Leading Lady),
Richard Wattis (the Leading Man) and Sheila
O'Neill (the Dancer).

221. *Above. Wait a Minim.* Fortune Theatre, 1964.
A South African musical revue, directed by Leon Gluckman, which featured native instruments and local colour.

222. *Below. At the Palace.* Palace Theatre, 1970.
By Barry Cryer, Dick Vosburgh and Bryan Blackburn, with music and lyrics by Bill Solly, directed by Freddie Carpenter.

'Fanny Oakley Rides again'—Toni Palmer (Calamity Jane), David Ellen (Marshall McLuhan), Danny La Rue (Fanny Oakley), Roy Hudd (Wild Bill Hickock) and Jackie Sands (Princess Morning Star).

223. *Right.* Danny La Rue *At the Palace*, wears Mark Canter's finale creation.

224. *Above. Oh! Calcutta!* 'An entertainment with music' devised by Kenneth Tynan. Royalty Theatre, 1970.
The opening parade, 'Taking off the robe', directed by Clifford Williams.

225. *Left.* 'One on One'. The *pas de deux* by Margo Sappington danced by Arlene Phillips and Jonathan Burn.

Revues which have run 250 performances and over in London 1893–1970

Note: Revues marked* were played twice daily or twice nightly, with matinées, hence the high number of performances.
The Follies was the first revue to run over 250 performances.

Name	Theatre and Date	Performances
BEYOND THE FRINGE	Fortune Theatre 10 May 1961	1,184
	Transferred to May Fair Theatre (Change of Director) 15 April 1964	1,016
	Total	2,200
* TOGETHER AGAIN	Victoria Palace 17 April 1947	1,566
* KNIGHTS OF MADNESS	Victoria Palace 16 March 1950	1,361
* LONDON LAUGHS	Adelphi Theatre 12 April 1952	1,113
* RING OUT THE BELLS	Victoria Palace 12 November 1952	987
* HAPPY AND GLORIOUS	London Palladium 3 October 1944	938
* JOKERS WILD	Victoria Palace 16 December 1954	911
* PARIS BY NIGHT	Prince of Wales' Theatre 9 April 1955	890
* THESE FOOLISH KINGS	Victoria Palace 18 December 1956	882
* FOLIES BERGERE REVUE	London Hippodrome 27 September 1949	881
SWEETER AND LOWER	Ambassadors Theatre 17 February 1944	870
* PARIS TO PICCADILLY	Prince of Wales' Theatre 12 April 1952	850
* PLEASURES OF PARIS	Prince of Wales' Theatre 20 April 1957	850
* CLOWN JEWELS	Victoria Palace 5 March 1959	803

Name	Theatre and Date	Performances
SWEETEST AND LOWEST	Ambassadors Theatre 9 May 1946	791
★ PICCADILLY HAYRIDE	Prince of Wales' Theatre 11 October 1946	778
AIRS ON A SHOESTRING	Royal Court Theatre 22 April 1953	772
★ PARDON MY FRENCH	Prince of Wales' Theatre 24 September 1953	758
★ JOY-BELLS!	London Hippodrome 25 March 1919	723
PLUME DE MA TANTE, LA	Garrick Theatre 3 November 1955	700
FOR AMUSEMENT ONLY	Apollo Theatre 5 June 1956	698
★ GET A LOAD OF THIS	London Hippodrome 19 November 1941	698
★ NIGHT AND THE MUSIC, THE	Coliseum 17 May 1945	686
★ STRIKE A NEW NOTE	Prince of Wales' Theatre 18 March 1943	661
★ TALK OF THE TOWN	Adelphi Theatre 17 November 1954	656
WAIT A MINIM!	Fortune Theatre 9 April 1964	656
★ STARLIGHT ROOF	London Hippodrome 23 October 1947	649
★ ZIG-ZAG!	London Hippodrome 31 January 1917	648
★ WHIRL OF THE WORLD, THE	London Palladium 14 March 1924	627
★ BOX O'TRICKS!	London Hippodrome 7 March 1918	625
★ BLACK VELVET	London Hippodrome 14 November 1939	620
BUZZ-BUZZ	Vaudeville Theatre 20 December 1918	612
★ BRIGHTER LONDON	London Hippodrome 28 March 1923	593
★ FOLIES BERGERE REVUE, 1951	London Hippodrome 6 March 1951	579

Name	Theatre and Date	Performances
* FINE FEATHERS	Prince of Wales' Theatre 11 October 1945	578
FOLLIES, THE	Apollo Theatre 1 December 1908	571
* HIGH TIME	London Palladium 20 April 1946	570
* TAKE IT FROM US	Adelphi Theatre 31 October 1950	570
PUNCH BOWL, THE	Duke of York's Theatre 21 May 1924	565
INTIMACY AT 8.30	Criterion Theatre 29 April 1954	551
* 1954 PALLADIUM SHOW, THE	London Palladium 5 May 1954	549
* SUCH IS LIFE	Adelphi Theatre 14 December 1955	548
FOLLIES, THE (revival)	Apollo Theatre 30 August 1910	521
CHARLOT'S REVUE (various editions)	Prince of Wales' Theatre 23 September 1924	518
CLOWNS IN CLOVER	Adelphi Theatre 1 December 1927	508
CO-OPTIMISTS, THE (1st season; various programmes)	Royalty Theatre 27 June 1921	500
* BEST BIB AND TUCKER	London Palladium 7 November 1942	490
* ROCKETS	London Palladium 25 February 1922	490
* HULLO, TANGO!	London Hippodrome 23 December 1913	485
CHEEP	Vaudeville Theatre 26 April 1917	483
* LEAP YEAR	London Hippodrome 20 March 1924	471
* ROUND IN FIFTY	London Hippodrome 16 March 1922	471
* IT'S FOOLISH, BUT IT'S FUN	Coliseum 12 March 1943	469
* LATIN QUARTER, 1951	London Casino 10 March 1951	468

Name	Theatre and Date	Performances
TAILS UP	Comedy Theatre 1 June 1918	467
★ HERE, THERE AND EVERYWHERE	London Palladium 4 April 1947	466
★ APPLE SAUCE (resumed run)	London Palladium 5 March 1941 (First produced Holborn Empire 27 August 1940, run interrupted by the Blitz)	462
★ LITTLE DOG LAUGHED, THE	London Palladium 11 October 1939	461
★ LATIN QUARTER, 1950	London Casino 18 March 1950	456
★ LATIN QUARTER	London Casino 19 March 1949	455
LYRIC REVUE, THE	Lyric Theatre, Hammersmith 24 May 1951 (Transferred to Globe Theatre 26 September 1951)	454
★ HULLO, RAG-TIME!	London Hippodrome 23 December 1912	451
GATE REVUE, THE	Ambassadors Theatre 9 March 1939	449
PENNY PLAIN	St. Martin's Theatre 28 June 1951	443
WHIRLIGIG, THE	Palace Theatre 23 December 1919	441
★ STRIKE IT AGAIN	Prince of Wales' Theatre 28 November 1944	438
★ BLUE MAGIC	Prince of Wales' Theatre 19 February 1959	436
★ YOU'LL BE LUCKY	Adelphi Theatre 25 February 1954	436
★ BLACK VANITIES	Victoria Palace 24 April 1941	435
AS YOU WERE	London Pavilion 3 August 1918	434
★ SAUCE TARTARE	Cambridge Theatre 18 May 1949	433
BUBBLY	Comedy Theatre 5 May 1917	429

Name	Theatre and Date	Performances
PIECES OF EIGHT	Apollo Theatre 23 September 1959	429
A TO Z	Prince of Wales' Theatre 21 October 1917	428
★ PEEP-SHOW, THE	London Hippodrome 14 April 1921	421
★ EXCITEMENT	London Casino 8 March 1952	419
LITTLE REVUE, THE	Little Theatre 21 April 1939	415
BRAN PIE	Prince of Wales' Theatre 28 August 1919	414
★ JOY-LAND!	London Hippodrome 23 December 1915	409
RAZZLE-DAZZLE	Theatre Royal, Drury Lane 19 June 1916	408
NINE SHARP	Little Theatre 26 January 1938	405
★ ROCKING THE TOWN	London Palladium 17 May 1956	397
BRIC-A-BRAC	Palace Theatre 18 September 1915	385
NINE O'CLOCK REVUE, THE	Little Theatre 25 October 1922	385
★ LARGE AS LIFE	London Palladium 23 May 1958	382
MORE (ODDS AND ENDS)	Ambassadors Theatre 18 June 1915	376
★ PAINTING THE TOWN	London Palladium 18 August 1955	373
LIVING FOR PLEASURE	Garrick Theatre 10 July 1958	370
★ FANCY FREE	Prince of Wales' Theatre 15 May 1951	
LONDON, PARIS, AND NEW YORK	London Pavilion 4 September 1920	366
★ HAW-HAW	Holborn Empire 22 December 1939	361
LEAGUE OF NOTIONS	New Oxford Theatre 17 January 1921	360

Name	Theatre and Date	Performances
★ PUSH AND GO	London Hippodrome 10 May 1915	359
HULLO AMERICA!	Palace Theatre 25 September 1918	358
SHEPHARD'S PIE	Princes Theatre 21 December 1939	356
EVERYBODY'S DOING IT	Empire Theatre 14 February 1912	354
★ STARS IN YOUR EYES	London Palladium 3 June 1960	354
★ TOUCH AND GO	Prince of Wales' Theatre 19 May 1950	352
FOR CRYING OUT LOUD	Stoll Theatre 6 August 1945	351
PASSING SHOW, THE	Palace Theatre 20 April 1914	351
★ LET'S FACE IT	London Hippodrome 19 November 1942	348
FINE AND DANDY	Saville Theatre 30 April 1942	346
★ WONDERFUL TIME	London Palladium 21 October 1952	344
★ SWINGING DOWN THE LANE	London Palladium 29 May 1959	343
BY-THE-WAY	Apollo Theatre 22 January 1925	341
HI-DE-HI	Palace Theatre 3 June 1943	340
JUST FANCY	Vaudeville Theatre 26 March 1920	333
UP AND DOING (resumed run)	Saville Theatre 20 May 1941 (First produced 17 April 1940 run interrupted by the blitz)	332
★ LA-DI-DA-DI-DA	Victoria Palace 30 March 1943	318
LONDON CALLING	Duke of York's Theatre 4 September 1923	316
THIS YEAR OF GRACE	London Pavilion 22 March 1928	316

Name	Theatre and Date	Performances
FOUR, FIVE, SIX	Duke of York's Theatre 11 March 1948	315
SHELL OUT	Comedy Theatre 24 August 1915	315
★ PALLADIUM PLEASURES	London Palladium 24 February 1926	312
U. S.	Ambassadors Theatre 28 November 1918	312
JIG-SAW!	London Hippodrome 14 June 1914	311
★ SKY HIGH	London Palladium 30 March 1925	306
★ NOT LIKELY!	Alhambra Theatre 4 May 1914	305
★ WE'RE HAVING A BALL	London Palladium 22 June 1957	305
SHARE MY LETTUCE	Lyric Theatre, Hammersmith 21 August 1957 (Transferred to Comedy Theatre 25 September 1957)	301
PELL-MELL	Ambassadors Theatre 5 June 1916	298
R.S.V.P.	Vaudeville Theatre 23 February 1926	297
BUSINESS AS USUAL	London Hippodrome 16 November 1914	295
FOR ADULTS ONLY	Strand Theatre 25 June 1958	292
SHOW'S THE THING, THE	Victoria Palace 4 June 1929	292
FUN AND GAMES	Princes Theatre 21 August 1941	289
PICK-A-DILLY	London Pavilion 18 April 1916	284
POT LUCK	Vaudeville Theatre 24 December 1921	284
BLACKBIRDS	London Pavilion 11 September 1926	279
WATCH YOUR STEP	Empire Theatre 4 May 1915	275

Name	Theatre and Date	Performances
TUPPENCE COLOURED	Globe Theatre 15 October 1947	274
SOME	Vaudeville Theatre 29 June 1916	273
COME OVER HERE	London Opera House (Stoll) 19 April 1913	271
YOU'D BE SURPRISED	Royal Opera House, Covent Garden 22 January 1923	271
YOICKS!	Kingsway Theatre 11 June 1924	271
HOUSE THAT JACK BUILT, THE	Adelphi Theatre 8 November 1929	270
TABS	Vaudeville Theatre 15 May 1918	268
VANITY FAIR	Palace Theatre 6 November 1916	265
SWEET AND LOW	Ambassadors Theatre 10 June 1943	264
WAKE UP AND DREAM	London Pavilion 27 March 1929	263
ODDS AND ENDS	Ambassadors Theatre 17 October 1914	259
RATS	Vaudeville Theatre 21 February 1923	258
FOLLY TO BE WISE	Piccadilly Theatre 8 January 1931	257
NEW FACES	Comedy Theatre 11 April 1940	257
HONI SOIT!	London Pavilion 6 September 1915	256
PUPPETS	Vaudeville Theatre 2 January 1924	255

Still Running 31 December 1970

Name	Theatre and Date	Performances
AT THE PALACE	Palace Theatre 9 April 1970	
OH! CALCUTTA!	The Round House 27 July to 19 September 1970 Royalty Theatre 30 September 1970	

INDEXES

REVUES ILLUSTRATED

SONGS, SKETCHES AND BALLETS

Way down East, 142
We'll go to church on Sunday,
83
When I am with her again, 61
When we were very young, 118

Who's the Lady?, 28
Who's Who, 209
Winter Fantasy, A, 74
World's Bazaar, The, 44
Wrong Bedroom, The, 212

Your lips say 'yes', 112

Zig-Zag Dance, The, 41

AUTHORS AND LYRICISTS

COMPOSERS

Quilter, Roger, 108

Rameau, 158
Redstone, Willy, 32
Rodgers, Richard, 118, 178

Sayer, Michael, 148
Scott, Cyril, 138
Sherwin, Manning, 176
Simpson, Fraser, 118
Solly, Bill, 202

Spurgin, Anthony, 148
Stamper, Dave, 60
Statham, Keith, 213
Strachey, Jack, 117
Sullivan, Henry, 153, 165
Swann, Donald, 197, 204

Tate, James W., 87, 90
Taylor, John, 220
Tierney, Harry, 33
Tilzer, Harry Von, 36

Trix, Helen, 115

Walker, William, 139, 162
Wallace, Edgar, 72
Walton, William, 164
Wimperis, Arthur, 44, 45, 46, 47
Wright, Geoffrey, 169, 192, 194

Zwar, Charles, 188, 195, 198, 219

PRODUCERS, DIRECTORS, CHOREOGRAPHERS

Albery, Bronson, 181
Anderson, John Murray, 78, 146
Arnold, Tom, 200
Ashton, Frederick, 164

Balanchine, George, 134
Black, Alfred, 208
Black, George, 166, 171, 183, 185, 208
Bridge, Peter, 220
Briggs, Hedley, 168
Butt, Alfred, 44, 47, 57, 62, 64

Carpenter, Freddie, 222
Chappell, William, 198, 199, 212, 220
Charlot, André, 30, 61, 66, 69, 77, 80, 93, 100-107, 119, 152, 153
Charnley, Michael, 205, 210
Cliff, Laddie, 83
Cochran, Charles B., 52, 71, 79, 81, 85, 89, 91, 92, 108, 114, 116, 120, 124, 133, 156, 163, 165, 174
Codron, Michael, 214

Day, Harry, 88
De Bear, Archibald, 83, 98, 117, 137, 149

De Courville, Albert, 23, 27, 49, 51, 55, 59, 72, 74, 112
De Valois, Ninette, 146
Dhéry, Robert, 207

Esdaile, Alfred, 161

Farjeon, Herbert, 162, 167, 168, 181
Farren, Fred, 39
Fazan, Eleanor, 213
French, Harold, 173

Gluckman, Leon, 221
Grattan, Henry, 52
Grossmith, George, 30

Henry, Charles, 88
Hickman, Charles, 188, 219
Hope, Vida, 206
Hulbert, Jack, 97, 123
Hurgon, Austen, 23
Hylton, Jack, 208

Kochno, Boris, 134
Kosloff, Theodore, 32

Laurillard, Edward, 97
Leslie, Lew, 92, 114

Leveaux, N. V., 30
Lister, Laurier, 192, 193, 197, 202
Littler, Emile, 200

Malone, J. A. E., 57
Marshall, Norman, 169, 195
Massine, Leonide, 108

Nesbitt, Robert, 200

Pélissier, H. G., 16, 17, 18
Pitt, Archie, 128, 142

Rodrigues, Alfred, 202
Rolls, Ernest C., 38

Sappington, Margot, 225
Shephard, Firth, 170, 175, 179, 195
Short, Hassard, 159

Tennent, H. M., 173, 198, 199, 212
Terriss, Tom, 10
Thomas, Stephen, 148
Tod, Quentin, 106, 107, 138

Wayburn, Ned, 37
Williams, Clifford, 224

DESIGNERS

Bakst, Léon, 27, 28
Beardsley, Aubrey, ('after'), 107
Beaton, Cecil, 164
Briggs, Hedley, 168

Calthrop, G. E., 189
Canter, Mark, 223
Chappell, William, 195

De Bethel, Joan and David, 206

Emmett, 192

Fougasse, 177

Hammond, Aubrey, 129
Hartnell, Norman, 172
Henri, Marc, 126
Hutton, Clark, 154

James, Charles, 158

Lancaster, Osbert, 197
Leverdet, 126

Messel, Oliver, 125

Molyneux, Edward, 96

Patou, Jean, 109
Piper, John, 209
Poiret, Paul, 71

Reville, 133
Rice, Peter, 212

Stowitts, 89
Sainthill, Loudon, 199

Zinkeisen, Doris, 160

ACTORS

Adrian, Max, 192, 194, 202, 204
Allan, Chesney, 166
Allandale, Ethel, 16, 17
Allen, Hilary, 198

Anderson, Lawrence, 159
Anthony, Michael, 195
Arnaw, Saffo, 36
Arnold, Marie, 113
Arundale, Sybil, 10, 12

Ashley, Iris, 149
Ashmole, Sylvia, 193
Attfield, Kitty, 101
Augarde, Amy, 56
Austin, Charles, 88

All talk at time is sense and folly blended:
Pity to look for sense where none's intended.

(Paraphrase from Montaigne Essays (Book II Chapter XII)